Love Notes

Creating love that lasts

Claire Gaudiani and David Burnett

LOVE NOTES
CREATING LOVE THAT LASTS

iUniverse books may be ordered through booksellers or by contacting:

iUniverse
1663 Liberty Drive
Bloomington, IN 47403
www.iuniverse.com
844-349-9409

ISBN: 978-1-6632-4995-1 (sc)
ISBN: 978-1-6632-4996-8 (e)

Print information available on the last page.

iUniverse rev. date: 02/13/2023

CONTENTS

PREFACE

As the first year of the pandemic rolled along, we realized that we had been together in our New York City apartment for many months on end. No visits from children or grandkids or trips to California to visit Claire's 99-year-old mother. No face-to-face bridge games played, no Confirmation classes taught in person, no church services attended, no trips to the grocery store, not even a hug from our beloved housekeeper/friend of many years.

And yet, we could honestly say that neither of us had felt a twinge of depression, loneliness, or frustration. Of course we missed all these wonderful people, the games and chocolate chips we had shared with grandkids many weekdays after school, but we still had each other and so life continued to feel whole.

The shared 'self' we had built over fifty plus years of marriage and defended fiercely through two careers, decades of parenting, and some serious physical challenges seemed well equipped to manage under such extreme conditions of isolation. Of course we recognized our financial and emotional security as primary assets, but how, exactly, were we able to retain a sense of joyfulness amid so many disturbing and complex challenges? We decided to have a try at understanding how our love protected and animated us for all those many months (and still does, for that matter!). You have the results of what we discovered in your hands. We learned a lot about what has sustained our relationship, not just in the past year, but over our shared lifetime. We hope you find our discoveries to be useful, and perhaps inspirational, in building your own joyful partnership with someone you love.

David and Claire

INTRODUCTION

Well, I've spent a lifetime lookin' for you;
singles bars and good time lovers were never true.
Playin' a fools game hopin' to win;
and tellin' those sweet lies and losin' again.
I was lookin' for love in all the wrong places,
Lookin' for love in too many faces,
searchin' their eyes and lookin' for traces
of what I'm dreamin' of.
Hopin' to find a friend and a lover;
I'll bless the day I discover
another heart lookin' for love.
"Lookin' for Love in All the Wrong Places"
(Mallette, Morrison and Ryan, 1980)

The search for love is as old as Adam and Eve. Advice about the search has been offered by old people to younger ones for almost as long. Is there really anything new to add at this point?

We feel empowered to give it a try. We have a special claim in this arena. We have achieved love over a period of 56 years together. It is sometimes awkward to admit how joyful and whole we feel as a couple. We do have the real thing, we believe, so why not try to tease out the elements that have worked for us? It is an enlightening process to undertake 'in retirement.' We sincerely hope that at least a few of our insights will prove useful to you in your search for the real thing, whether you are seeking a partner or have already launched a shared search within the joys of coupledom.

Love as a category is a big bucket. It is regularly used to describe people's relationship to their children, parents, friends, pets, country and/or fellow human beings in general. These are powerful and important relationships, and they do offer opportunities for insight into the nature of 'real' love with a chosen partner. The love of a parent for a child, for instance, illustrates a kind of selfless, all-encompassing sentiment that defies rational boundaries. Remember the famous parable from the Christian Bible about the 'prodigal son'?[1] A wealthy father has two sons. The younger one is impatient to make his way in the world and asks for his 'inheritance' in advance. His father accedes to this extraordinary request and off goes the kid to live the high life in a new land. Of course he wastes his fortune in short order and when famine strikes, he is reduced to begging for work. He gets work, all right, tending swine and dreaming about eating the awful stuff he feeds his charges.

He finally wakes up to his circumstances and heads back home where he hopes for menial work among his father's slaves, knowing that he has foolishly sacrificed his standing as his father's son. Upon arrival, however, he is embraced by his joyful father who covers him with fine clothes, puts a ring on his finger, and throws a banquet to celebrate his return. Needless to say, this does not sit well with the dutiful older brother, who has spent his years following all the rules of the household. He has never gotten, as he bitterly points out, even a goat to party with his friends. He also notes that his kid brother is a wastrel who hangs with

---

[1] Luke 15:11–32.

prostitutes (not clear how he knows this) and deserves nothing. Welcome home, bro!

It is left to the father to explain what things look like through the lens of 'real love.' "Everything I have is yours," he tells the older son. "But your brother was lost" ('dead' in the father's terminology), "and now has come back to life! What's not to celebrate?" Nothing is too good for his boys. He is not in the business of passing judgments or measuring the merits of one son against the other.

His boys, however, are not on the same sheet of music. BOTH of them are operating in a transactional universe of an eye for an eye, or crime and punishment, or whatever you like. The younger son expects to be judged and punished and even ostracized for his selfish behavior. The older son expects the appropriate rewards for following all the rules and is anxious to score points by comparing his actions to those of his brother. Each is equally clueless about how real (transcendent) love works.

The father's love is all-encompassing and unwavering, outside the boundaries of time and space, and unconnected to any particular action or event. There is no scorecard; there are no winning or losing transactions; there is no barometer to measure how such love rises or falls according to any behavior on the part of either son. This form of love generates security and joyfulness that surpasses any rational explanation. It is a pretty good model for the 'real' love that two unrelated people set out to build when they elect to pledge their lives to one another.

We will encounter this distinction between transactional behavior and transcendent behavior frequently as we explore the building of a loving relationship with someone who began life as a stranger to you. It is not that one of these forms of behavior is good and the other bad. Rather, we will make the case that when one form dominates the other, individuals are less able to build a loving partnership. We feel we have achieved 'real' love. We are still two individuals, but frankly, it is difficult to distinguish where one of us ends and the other begins. We are a bigger and better version of ourselves than would be possible on our own. We feel joyful, a condition that surpasses happiness and brings stability, security and energy to our coupledom. We are indivisible, two in one. The concept is difficult to grasp, given how deeply most of us are locked into our individual, material 'selves.'

We can appreciate that many readers/listeners might quickly respond to our cheerful claims with the thought "so what?" Circumstances differ for every person and every couple. What might a couple of old, white hetero married people have to say about love that would be useful to me? To which we can only respond, "fair enough." We know how difficult it is to find a trustworthy, experienced and relevant source of advice or feedback at any place or time. And we are well aware that finding a competent, committed partner among the billions of strangers across the world is much more challenging than loving children with whom you share flesh and blood. And you are right to be cautious, given how much bad and self-serving advice is floating around out there in the ether. On the other hand, our desire to share our experience is sincere and there is little to lose in investigating such an important topic.

We don't mean to be frivolous, but perhaps you can think of your investment of time with us in the same way that Blaise Pascal, the seventeenth-century French mathematician, thought about believing in the existence of God. To believe, he argued, was the only rational strategy. There was no way to know one way or the other. So why not? If God ultimately turned out not to exist, believing had cost you little, other than time spent in worship and in good deeds during your time on earth. If God did exist on the other hand, you, as a believer, would hit the jackpot in the afterlife. And if you had decided not to believe, and God turned out to exist after all, you'd be left hoping for mercy! Betting on the existence of God was a 'no-brainer' in Pascal's judgment.[2]

Speaking of God, you may have already noticed that we are using some pretty slippery words to describe this state of 'love' we are claiming as our own. Things like 'shared state of being' and 'joyful indivisibility' do not always go down well with materially oriented folks. It is evident to us, however, that the connections we have built with one another over the decades do transcend our physical existence. These bonds defy the rational limits of our 'minds,' that is, our reasoning selves. So, in order to talk about our relationship, we will need to discuss a third dimension of human existence beyond the mind and body, specifically, the spiritual self. We want to clarify that the 'spirit,' in our usage, should not be confused with spirituality in the sense of adherence to an organized religion. We are a mixed marriage when it comes to the existence of God. A believer and an agnostic. What we have to say does not assume a willingness to embrace a religious faith. It does require a belief in the power of love to create a dimension of existence that is intangible, irrational, and absolutely real. We call it a transcendent relationship, to distinguish from the transactional nature of most human interactions. Here is how Claire thinks about the value that organized religion can add to the search for love:

---

[2] Blaise Pascal (1623–1662) was a French mathematician and philosopher best known for his collected *Thoughts* (*Les Pensées*), where his description of 'betting' on the existence of God is found in several variations. There is an excellent summary of Pascal's wager in the *Stanford Encyclopedia of Philosophy*.

Our secular society tends to link spirituality solely with religions and religious institutions. I have tended not to have such high expectations of religious leaders of my time. They are profoundly human; thus they are more or less weak individuals, like all of us. Many may be trying to achieve special levels of virtue. Many succeed. But all of them, like the human institutions they lead, are deeply flawed.

Nevertheless, over thousands of years, religions have produced and preserved great texts, values and practices. This wisdom tradition can comfort and strengthen all people on the journey from childhood to adulthood. The error is to confuse this priceless heritage with the failures and disappointments of religious leaders. I have been so grateful to be a social justice Roman Catholic all my life. The sacraments, the Saints, the practices and celebrations of the communities I have belonged to have helped me become a better version of myself, and thus a better partner for David. So I dearly hope that any of our readers who can't tolerate organized religion will read on to explore with us how adults can weave more joy into their everyday lives.

Hopefully you agree that the parable of the prodigal son illustrates this important 'wisdom tradition' among organized religions. We also wish to acknowledge our debt to the British writer/scholar C.S. Lewis, whose writings inspired us to undertake this project.[3]

---

[3] C.S. Lewis (1898–1963) is an English author perhaps best known for *The Chronicles of Narnia*, his fantasy classic. He was a fellow in English Literature at Oxford University and later the Chair of Medieval and Renaissance

The Screwtape Letters, written in the early 1940s, is not a product of organized religion, nor is it a traditional self-help book. There are no aphorisms to live by or seven habits to memorize. It's a compendium of thirty letters from a senior devil named Screwtape (senior in the 'lowerarchy' of Hell) to a junior devil-in-training named Wormwood.

Wormwood's job in the netherworld is to capture the soul (the spirit?) of the human 'patient' to whom he is assigned, in this case an Englishman in his 20s who is anxious to leave his mother's home, find a bride, and begin an independent life. But the junior devil makes endless 'rookie' mistakes while attempting to lead his patient astray. His inexperience with human vulnerabilities is evident. The exasperated (and very funny) letters from his supervisor, Screwtape, critique his trainee's missed opportunities and miscalculations. The result is a compendium of human foibles, weaknesses, and blind spots as seen through the eyes of an experienced devil, well-practiced in the arts of seducing humans away from a generous and fulfilling life, and thus from any chance of a loving relationship with another human. Screwtape is selfish, aggressive, subtle, impatient, and utterly subversive. In short he is perfectly devilish, the polar opposite of the best version of the 'patient.'

In one particular letter, Screwtape lectures Wormwood on the self-deception that characterizes humans who think they are 'in love.' Humans beings, explains Screwtape, frequently use 'love' to justify misguided and often destructive behavior (just what the devils have in mind for us). Humans proclaim that they were/are

---

Literature at Cambridge and a prolific writer of literary criticism, essays of all sorts, and many volumes on Christianity, Before, during, and after WWII, Lewis was a prominent public intellectual, writing for magazines and newspapers and appearing regularly on radio. In fact, *The Screwtape Letters* appeared as a column in *The Guardian* during the years 1940-41.

so smitten that they have lost their ability to act rationally. They justify extravagant commitments or changes in behavior in the name of love, although they are actually living the experience of 'falling in love' which bears little relationship to the real thing. Falling in love is an emotional high driven by a lot of hormones. The 'real thing' is the product of years of mutual investment in one another. It is an end result. Humans regularly confuse these two very different experiences with one another and confuse themselves in the process. The devils approve mightily of this kind of self-deception. In fact, Screwtape takes credit for creating such deception. It is one of his favorite moves to ensure that humans live in disappointment (and thus separated from their Creator) because of their own misguided expectations.

Aha! said we. Pretty clever! We certainly thought we had 'found love' when we met and married. But, in retrospect, we were definitely operating on emotional fumes! Our best thinking involved taking all the money we had in the world (less than $2,000) and traveling through Europe for three months in a rental car. More about all this later, but what must our parents have thought? We survived ninety uninterrupted days of one-on-one togetherness and claimed the experience as a 'building block' for a life together! At the outset, we were probably more lucky than good at marriage. A marriage license can look more like a hunting license, a permit to begin the hunt for real love, the 'coupledom' that can only be achieved over decades.

Are you having another "so what?" moment? Well, hang on… Exaggerated expectations about achieving love overnight are potentially harmful to one's ability to invest in a relationship, to change, pivot, reset, and restart, over and over. Unrealistic expectations that go unnoticed are a serious impediment to building a happy and generous life. They are a clear example of self-deception, that greatest of all human weaknesses. Our penchant for believing what we want to believe, about ourselves and others, is a serious barrier to building good relationships.

Think about it. How well do you practice self-awareness and self-management? How often do you honestly and carefully assess your own motivations? Do you ever get off track? Do you actually have a track to get off in the first place? Any idea about a 'best version' of your self? Did you pick up any skills to deal with such questions around the family dinner table? In school? In church? On a night out with the guys/gals? Yet self-awareness constitutes the best defense against the wiles of the devils seeking your descent into self-centered loneliness. Only self-analytical people can understand and capitalize on their agency, that powerful combination of will, energy, confidence and conviction that enables them to define the trajectory of their lives, even when 'fate' seems to work against them. In retrospect, we recognize some of the strengths that helped us turn our hunting license into a shared self, and we thank C.S. Lewis for the inspiration to look at our own anti-devil tactics.

Is Lewis's insight about 'falling in love' versus 'real' love original? Not exactly. Is it a quick fix for what may depress you? Probably not. But is it wise to think of love as where you are headed rather than where you are now or want to be tomorrow? We would say that this is the essential starting point for a loving partnership. It is equally wise to remember that everyone and everything changes over time and thus relationships (and expectations) must change as well, constantly. *The Screwtape Letters* offers a great look in the mirror at the many human weaknesses we all deal with every day. We can't promise to be as witty or profound as Lewis is, but we hope to help you discover a few weapons against Satan's foot soldiers in the following speculations.

And, by the way, as a reminder of what 'real' love looks like, no matter your cultural or religious background, you can do no better than to recall the passage from I Corinthians in the Christian Bible so frequently cited at Christian weddings.[4] For starters, as you embark on some thinking about yourself, try replacing the word 'love' in these declarations with your own name and see how they sound:

Love is patient
Love is kind.
Love is not jealous.
Love is not boastful.
Love is not rude.
Love is not arrogant.
Love is not irritable.
Love is not resentful.
Love does not insist on its own way.
Love does not rejoice at wrongs.
Love bears all things, believes all things,
hopes all things, endures all things.
Love never ends.

Hmmm…and the supreme test…if you have a partner, try inserting both names!

Don't worry! There are no perfect scores in the game of life! What matters is a commitment to becoming a more loving and loveable partner. That will require an endless succession of resets and do-overs and pivots because life, and people, are unpredictable. In order to carry out such maneuvers, you need a clear understanding of your 'self.' In Part One, we take a look at the elements that make up a 'self,' and the unique human abilities you have available to manage your 'self.' The ideal outcome is a self that you like

---

[4] I Corinthians 13:4–8.

living with who controls the meaning of whatever events fate has to offer. We then devote a chapter to self-deception, the widespread problem that threatens our self-understanding (and our prospects for long term love).

We conclude Part One with a brief assessment of our own levels of self-understanding when we met as two individual strangers almost sixty years ago. Talk about low test scores! And, of course, we encourage you to do a bit of assessment as well.

In Part Two of *Love Notes*, we explore what we call 'coupledom,' that is the process of merging two 'selfs' into a single shared entity over time. We look at the 'habits of mind' that will enable this process to succeed, focusing on three complicated but critical areas: humor, attention and imagination. And we conclude in our final chapter with an examination of several serious inflection points in our life together, moments when we were tested by fate and by our own shortcomings.

Our 'habits of mind,' we believe, pulled us through those moments and strengthened our shared bond. We also learned that 'real love' generates concern and caring, not just for each other and our immediate family, but also for others. There is a kind of halo effect that is larger than our own shared love for one another. So, as part of our ongoing effort to increase our generosity toward others, we have thought hard about our own experiences in the hope that we could identify ideas of value to others who are in the earlier stages of building a loving life together. It will be up to you to judge whether we have succeeded.

PART ONE

What About You?
What About (Each Of) Us?

CHAPTER ONE

Building A Loving And Loveable Self

Not everything that can be counted counts and
not everything that counts can be counted.
Albert Einstein

We believe that everyone has the potential to create a long term
loving relationship with another human. It's not easy and it's not
quick but it can be done. The starting point is to develop your
'self' before you embark on the journey to partnership.

It is a given that you need to care for and care about yourself in
order to become a good partner. You must create a person that you
genuinely like and enjoy living with. You must cultivate a sense of
self-worth, because no one can supply this fundamental asset for
you. Given our remarkable capacity for self-awareness, we all live
with our 'self' 24 hours a day. Don't love yourself? Unlikely that
others will. So you need to think carefully about your 'self,' your
expectations, your priorities, your motives and your behavior. In
short, you need a level of self-understanding to engage seriously in
the journey toward a transcendent love of another human being.

1

And you will need to continue to revisit your 'self' on a regular basis. An unexamined life is not worth living, as Plato said. We will focus first on the powers you have to understand yourself, to keep things headed in the right direction, and to 'course correct' when things get off track. Ultimately the ideal is a strong sense of your self, your personal ability to define the meaning of events in your life, and thus to be prepared to contribute to a strong partnership.

Please do not get the idea that we are oblivious to the struggles of loving and caring for oneself. We understand that millions of people of all ages face great challenges trying to achieve a healthy level of self-care for many reasons. We also understand that in some religions, such as Buddhism, this is the project that drives their adherence to their faith. We are clearly not professional psychologists, nor do we mean to be presumptuous in dispensing advice about how you or anyone else should build a 'self.' This is simply a reflection on our experience as a couple of reasonably sane, optimistic people who are well aware of the many privileges we have enjoyed over a lifetime.

Here is a brief case study that illustrates the challenges we are talking about and some of the mistakes that well-educated people can make. This (edited) letter to the editor of *T Magazine* [5] is seeking advice from its 'cultural therapist.' The writer signed off as 'Name Withheld.'

> I have a problem. I'm nearly 40 and I find myself
> at a crossroads that feels more like a dead end. I've
> spent much of my life and thought and income in
> pursuit of beauty in one form or another: design,

[5] This letter appeared in *T Magazine* on December 30, 2019 in an article entitled "How Do I Find Meaning and Beauty in My Life?" *T Magazine* focusses on arts and culture and is published by the *New York Times*.

fashion, the beauty or 'wellness' industries. This is very much a professional hazard: My career in glossy magazines and advertising as a photo editor is all about making beautiful images of beautiful things that I've selected look even more beautiful. Often, when I think how much of my time I've devoted to my own appearance or to matters of aesthetics, I cringe.

I've come to a place in which I no longer know what my own life should look like. I literally do not know what to do with myself and what I should believe in anymore... My standard of living hasn't flourished. I'm unable to save money for retirement and... I've lost my sense of meaning to myself.

I feel alone in many ways and unsuccessful by most measures. I don't own a home and no one needs me. My friends and peers have gone on to have families, to marry and to stop working or have moved even to foreign countries.

I am accountable to no one but myself. On good days, I can take a yoga class and still feel life's potential. On bad ones, I feel such futility like I've squandered my youth. Am I simply being solipsistic here? Or is this what getting older is about, acknowledging one's comedown to the brutal reality of life?

Let's assume for the moment that the writer is female, although maybe not?? This plea, whether real or composed by some clever editor, struck us as both touching and tragic. It brings together many threads we have encountered in conversations with people the ages of our children, and it piqued our curiosity about how we got to where we are. Does 'Name Withheld' seem ready to embark on building a robust enduring relationship with another adult? Does she in fact have a 'self' to bring to a partnership? What could she do to 'reset' at this low point in her life? If you are curious, you are welcome to jump to the Appendix of *Love Notes* where you will find our response to 'Name Withheld.' Or you may wish to follow along with our broader analysis of the 'self' and then consider what you would say to her. In either case, keep her in mind as we discuss the limitations of a transactional mindset and the importance of the idea of beauty in everyone's life.

How does one start thinking about the idea of a 'self' in the first place? This question has preoccupied some of the greatest thinkers for millennia, from Aristotle to Freud, from Augustine to Descartes. We don't claim expertise to discuss the merits of the many competing concepts, so we will instead adapt a straightforward proposition by a Roman poet. Seems wonky, but we will move quickly, we promise. Juvenal set out his idea two thousand years ago[6]—"Mens sana in corpore sano"—a healthy mind in a healthy body. You've heard that one before and it remains a fine ideal to shoot for. But Juvenal isn't quite finished. He adds a third dimension at the end of his poem:

> semita certe, tranquillae per
> virtutem patet unica vitae.
> (certainly the only road to a life of
> peace/satisfaction is virtue)

The Latin word 'virtu' conveys a larger idea than the English

---

[6] In Satire X, composed in the late first or early second century.

word 'virtue.'[7] It means more than choosing right over wrong or following a set of moral precepts. 'Virtu' refers to a way of being in the world that engages more than your physical being and your rational 'mind.' Maybe 'character' would be a better translation. It invokes what we are calling 'spirit,' our human capacity to think and act in terms that 'transcend' both reason and physicality. The joy we can experience through love cannot be fully explained by rational or physical processes. It is a manifestation of our spirit, the third dimension of the self that must be nurtured and activated, just as we mobilize our bodies and our minds. Think, for example, of the state of mind evoked by an act of generosity or kindness, or by an encounter with a beautiful sunset. Such moments offer a 'glimpse' of a larger universe that cannot be described in purely rational or physical terms.

The existence of a spiritual self is central to our concept of love. In the Hebrew Bible, the prophets portray justice in terms of an eye for an eye, a tooth for a tooth. Justice is 'proportional' and meted out in transactional terms. Prophets argued that a messiah would arrive to make final judgments. Meanwhile, a lot of rules and laws created by humans had to be followed, as is usually the case when some humans get into positions of authority over other humans. When an unexpected kind of messiah did arrive, a very different view of justice followed. Jesus argued, as did the early prophets, that there would be a final judgment day, but he asserted that it would be based on *love!* even of one's enemy. He assured his followers that they would be rewarded if they behaved counter-intuitively in loving (all) their neighbors (as themselves). The 'rules' were not the deciding factor. By believing him, his

---

[7] For a lengthy list of 'virtues' from religious and secular sources, see https://www.detroitcatholic.com/news/world-has-rich-tradition-of-elucidating-virtues-principles-for-way-to-live. For our purposes, we intend a general meaning of 'a way of being in the world' rather than a specific behavior or action.

disciples would share the power to love beyond themselves and achieve 'joyfulness' in the process.

Whether you are a disciple or not, the contrast in pre-Christian and Christian worldviews challenges you to form an operating plan for your 'self' in the world. Do you engage your 'spirit,' your non-transactional, non-material self, in your actions or not? Here is an illustration of empowering one's spirit as an equal partner with human rationality. Consider the Truth and Reconciliation Commission in South Africa in the 1990s, in contrast with the war crimes tribunals (the so-called Nuremberg Trials) in Germany after World War II. In the latter case, the purpose was to administer social/civic justice. This required assembling evidence of wrongdoing beyond a reasonable doubt, identifying and convicting the wrongdoers and finally imposing 'punishment' to fit the heinous crimes against humanity committed by the Nazis.

The goal of the Truth and Reconciliation Commission was to identify and acknowledge the heinous behaviors of white leaders during the era of apartheid in South Africa. Individuals were invited to admit voluntarily to their actions, to accept responsibility and to ask for forgiveness. The victims of these crimes were called upon to forgive the perpetrators, to reconcile with them and with the larger society. When the process was completed, there were no further consequences in terms of retribution or restitution. Humans mobilized their spiritual selves in support of a greater good. They trusted that together they had the power to reset, not to hide the past but to acknowledge it and create a new future. How well did it work? That is a difficult question when considered at the societal level. But the courageous actions of those individuals directly involved in the process set a standard for human behavior that affirmed our capacity to operate beyond the transactional.[8]

The relative rarity of efforts such as the Commission in South Africa underscores the difficulty of operating in a spiritual dimension. There is no point in minimizing the challenges we all face when trying to get to love. Humans are, for instance, remarkably poor at analyzing our own wants and needs accurately. Even when we try to act generously, we often conceal from ourselves the truth of our motivations. It is not difficult to identify situations in which people in positions of power or authority act in their own self-interest, rather than in the best interests of those for whom they are responsible. Examples abound over the history of religious institutions, governments, businesses, and, of course, marriages. And humans may well do so while professing (and perhaps believing) that they are acting generously. Nevertheless, we offer this illustration so you can understand our belief in the necessity of including your 'spirit' in your efforts to create a loving and loveable self. We have more to say about the problem of self-deception in a following chapter.

This three-part scheme—body, mind, and spirit—provides a useful, if imperfect, way to discuss the 'self.' We ask you to accept this framework in the interest of advancing our discussion of love. It is a big simplification and must not be taken literally. Your physical being (and for discussion purposes we are including your 'feelings/emotions/sentiments' as part of the physical domain), your logical mind and your spirit are not distinct or independent elements. They are interdependent and indivisible. All three dimensions require nurture and care to support one another and all play an important role in the management of the self.

---

[8] The voluminous report of the South African TRC (1995–2002) is online at www.justice.gov.za. Canada implemented a similar commission in 2008 to address the nation's dealings with Indigenous peoples.

But it is useful to think about different kinds of investments to strengthen these different elements of the self. We strengthen our minds and reasoning abilities through education and the study of formal systems (such as language or mathematics). We care for our bodies through nourishment, hygiene (physical and mental) and exercise. Between the Soul Cycle outpost on the corner, and the large fridge in the kitchen, and that luxurious oversized spa/ bathroom you covet, body care is frequently front and center in our consciousness.

Spirit does not always get its own 'spa treatment,' although like any muscle, if you don't use it regularly, it can weaken and eventually atrophy. A spiritual self requires regular workouts to be an active part of your life. And, to clarify once again, we do not see spirituality and religion as the same thing. In our mind, religion is an institutional organization, for the purpose of attracting and sustaining commitment to a particular system of belief, a 'creed' if you will. Spirituality is your personal capacity to glimpse and engage your 'self' in a reality beyond the finite, transactional world.

CHAPTER TWO

Three Assets For Investing In Your (Spiritual) Self

What exactly does an investment in one's spiritual 'self' look like? How to nurture those intangible qualities of virtue and character? Those special human abilities such as self-analysis or an appreciation of beauty? These elements are essential to making love a durable reality, rather than a simple emotional high. They will be called on throughout your (love) life. Without a robust spirit, life can (and will) devolve into a succession of transactions: finite, predictable, uninspiring and, ultimately, unfulfilling—just what 'Name Withheld' is facing.

Investing in your spiritual self is challenging, as C.S. Lewis points out so entertainingly. Both our human 'nature' and the world we live in present challenges that push us toward self-centeredness and transactional operating principles. Whatever your age, you are naturally influenced by the Darwinian need for survival. Your instincts (some use the delightful term 'reptilian brain') make you into what economists have dubbed 'homo economicus.' You operate frequently as a self-optimizing, transactional creature in the zero-sum world. You often think, if not act, using a kind of

Old Testament, 'eye for an eye,' calculus. Your instincts do not automatically embrace the joys of delayed gratification, empathy or forgiveness. Like all of us, you are materially-oriented, self-centered and shortsighted.

You are also, according to psychologists, built to see the worst coming and to act accordingly. The technical term is 'negativity bias,' meaning that your 'gator brain' (easier to remember than reptilian) finds loss to be much more painful than gain is joyful. This behavior is also based in our evolutionary survival needs. But a series of negative experiences can quickly lead to an emotional, and often pessimistic, mindset that prevents you from controlling your reactions to events.

Top this off with a tendency to deceive ourselves about what our real motivations are, add in the stresses of career building, a few strong and potentially confusing external influences from well-meaning friends, family members, and social media, as well as a pandemic for good measure, and it doesn't take long to see what you are up against, especially when dealing with a high risk proposition like preparing to trust and respect another human being for a lifetime.

Despite these fundamental challenges, you have at least some valuable assets at your disposal. If you are reading this, chances are you have a good education, reasonable physical health, at least an average income, and a modest degree of security. You also enjoy a degree of personal freedom resulting from these factors and your citizenship in a reasonably democratic society. Most importantly you have several powers available to combat these negative influences and enhance your spirit. The first is your 'free will' (your ability to make judgments and decisions). The second is your 'consciousness' (the ability to reflect on your own behavior, analyze your decisions and 'change your mind' as often as needed);

and the third power is your 'conscience' (the capacity to evaluate your decisions on a moral level). Let's see what happens when you mobilize these powerful abilities.

ASSET ONE: FREE WILL

You possess the power to make decisions for better or worse. Although genomics has extended our understanding of the operating instructions we are born with in our genes, even the most ardent materialists have failed to demonstrate that any of our actions are 'predestined.' There is no 'string puller,' cosmic or otherwise, making you do stuff. You have the power to frame your priorities and to act accordingly. You have what we are calling agency, the power to define the meaning (at least in your life) of events that occur, even when things do not go according to 'plan.' We all know, thanks to Jimmy Carter, that life is not fair. Some circumstances and experiences are challenging or worse. But such influences do not actually control your decisions. How strong your agency is will be a product of your investments in your self. Making intelligent decisions based on the powers of the mind/ body/spirit triad will, at a minimum, strengthen your ability to deal with any outcome, good or bad. You will be confident that you have brought your best effort to the challenge and are prepared to deal constructively with its consequences.

Here is an illustration of the importance of free will in the building of agency. The men who drafted the American 'creed' wrote about the individual search for what they called 'happiness.' Remember the Declaration of Independence? "[all men] are endowed by their Creator with certain unalienable Rights… to Life, Liberty and the pursuit of Happiness."

The wording is very precise. There is a 'right to life' and a 'right to liberty' but there is no 'right to happiness.' The key word here

11

is *pursuit.* Happiness is the result of a quest. It is not delivered to anyone by anyone. It is not found by accident along the side of the road. It is a product of individual choices. The Founders believed that this quest, guided by individual free will, was a fundamental human right. They felt that no government should control individual decision-making. No citizen would be referred to as a 'subject' (by implication, someone less than free). We recognize that this 'self-evident' truth excluded many, many groups and individuals at the time of its writing. The project to extend these 'unalienable rights' to all men/people is ongoing.

Free will does, however, oblige us to create ourselves through our decisions, a circumstance that has been seen alternately as a curse or a blessing throughout the ages.[9] In a Christian context, C.S. Lewis deploys his usual skilled reasoning:

> God created a thing that had free will. That means creatures which can go wrong or right. Some people think they can imagine a creature which was free but had no possibility of going wrong, but I can't. If a thing is free to be good, it's also free to be bad. And free will is what has made evil possible (...). Why then did God give them free will? Because free will, though it makes evil possible, is also the only thing that makes possible any love or goodness or joy worth having.[10]

---

[9] The burden of freedom was a popular topic in the mid-twentieth century, giving rise to such existentialist classics as *The Plague* by Albert Camus and *No Exit* by Jean-Paul Sartre. Camus' essay *The Myth of Sisyphus* defines the challenge of coping with the uncertainties of fate. Existentialist writers also worried about the burden of consciousness, that is, our ability, for better or worse, to see ourselves and judge our actions.

[10] *The Case for Christianity* (1943).

And that is the point. Free will is essential to real love, with or without a divinity. But with such awesome opportunity comes the potential for bad choices. And this is where we get into our responsibility to make decisions and live with their consequences. The power to make decisions is essential, but as they say, decisions have consequences, so we next need to consider the power available to assess your decisions. Making no decision is a decision, but ignoring the entire question about a moral dimension in your decisions is clear neglect of the spirit.

ASSET TWO: CONSCIOUSNESS/SELF-AWARENESS

Consciousness is the human secret sauce, the mystery of the 'self.' For our purposes, happily, we do not feel obliged to deal with the origins of consciousness, which is one tough nut to crack. But each of us can 'see' ourselves in action quite clearly; we act and see ourselves acting at the same time. When you invoke this power of (self)-consciousness, you can reflect on your own thoughts and actions; you can assess yourself. In fact, you are obliged to do so even when you would prefer to avoid such responsibility. Such frivolous credos as "I make it up as I go along," or "I just live day to day" are not worthy of individuals seeking lasting relationships.

Consciousness, for instance, enables you to identify the influences at work in your decision-making. Your 'mind,' i.e. your reason, may well compete with your emotions; your 'body' may want 'x' while your mind and/or spirit would prefer 'y.' You can ask yourself why this is the case. And, very importantly, you can ask why you chose a particular way forward at a given moment. You can 'see' the power of instinctive behavior in your work life, as in those cases where you (perhaps unthinkingly) choose the outcome that is most advantageous to you personally (rational, self-optimizing behavior). Likewise, you can identify those moments when you are perhaps influenced by a particular friend, mentor or prior experience. When such reflection is carried out consistently and carefully, you will be well-positioned to take responsibility for your decisions. You need only combine your self-awareness with your conscience.

ASSET THREE: CONSCIENCE

Your conscience enables a third step in the process of self-understanding beyond simply making a decision and reflecting on it. You can assess the moral value of your decisions. This ensures that the non-rational, non-material (spiritual) dimension of your action is given equal attention in your self-consideration. The idea that humans possess some kind of innate moral framework is often conflated with traditional religious teachings. Free will means you can 'sin' if you like. You want to go for what the snake has to offer?? Go for it, just as Eve did! Such a Biblical reference implies that humans know what is 'right and wrong' directly from God. Perhaps so, but there is plenty of evidence that every 'civilization' across the globe from our earliest origins established taboos, or unacceptable behaviors, long before the organization of formal religions. For instance, no evidence exists of a culture on earth that deemed it praiseworthy to 'steal' something belonging to another, whether a knife, a horse or a woman. Has there ever been a society where members did not steal from one another? Absolutely not. People knew it was wrong and did it anyway. Did they really 'know' that it was wrong to steal or kill wantonly? No way to survey the Neanderthals, but when you think about it, the idea of a 'conscience' is pretty intuitive.

How do you recognize bad behavior on your own part or in the world in general? Because you 'know' goodness. Evil has no meaning on its own. It only exists in relation to something else, i.e. the behavior characterized as good, generous, kind, trustworthy, brave, etc. Free will gives you the power to choose wrong over right, even when you know the difference. This is a pretty straightforward explanation for why there seems to be so much evil in the world. This view inspired G.K. Chesterton to produce one of the great witticisms of all time: "Original sin… is the only part of Christian theology which can really be proved."[11] How great is that line?!

When conscience is activated, your decision-making is not limited to physical and rational dimensions. It is not limited to the transactional universe. You will need to animate a bigger self to get to love. Love requires an ability to embrace the idea of a 'greater good' than yourself. For certain you will need to enrich your playbook to include ways of living and being that are not simply transactional. If you find yourself thinking primarily in terms of giving and getting, of doing this to obtain that, there is some work to do to animate your spiritual self.

So there, at a very high level, is a sketch of a human self, a composite of mind, body, and spirit endowed with free will, consciousness, and a conscience. When these components are high functioning, they create 'agency.' This term defines our ability to operate in the world with personal responsibility, purpose, and priorities. Agency generates our ability to deal with the unpredictable and randomness of events beyond our control. However, as C.S. Lewis dramatizes so effectively, there exists a persistent challenge that we all face in developing our best selves and that is self-deception. *Self-deception is the enemy of personal agency.* We have the tools to see ourselves in action, to assess our behavior, and to change course as we see fit. But it is not a simple or easy or 'natural' process for an individual. *The Screwtape Letters* provides a catalogue of challenges to overcome in this effort. The letter to the editor from 'Name Withheld' is likewise filled with warnings about how and where self-deception may arise.

---

[11] Gilbert Keith Chesterton, *Orthodoxy*, originally published in 1908.

CHAPTER THREE

Self-Deception: The Challenge To A Loveable Self

'Name Withheld,' you will recall, deceived herself about the rewards of her career. She clearly expected her work life to provide a key source of personal fulfillment. We are hardly the first ones to point out that this proposition is both common and misguided.[12] Success in work life often means chasing the next promotion or the next set of goals into an inevitable rat race. It is a transactional pursuit. Work life is certainly important to developing a sense of self-worth, but it is not the pathway to becoming a loveable self. 'Name' has unconsciously trapped herself in a narrow framework and lost contact with her spiritual self.

This example reveals a major element at work in the human psyche that contributes to the commonality of self-deception. We are built to develop habits of mind and body, i.e. ways of doing things that require minimal thought or reflection. The result is efficient use of time and brain power. But habits obey one of the basic laws of physics, momentum. Any object, when energy is

---

[12] See David Brooks' opinion piece entitled "Five Lies" in the *New York Times*, April 15, 2019.

applied to it, is put into motion in a certain direction. On a pool table, the cue ball 'wants to' continue indefinitely in the exact direction of its launch by the pool cue. To cause the ball to change direction, it is necessary to apply energy once again, by hitting it with another ball, etc. Once a habit is 'launched,' it requires energy to change it. It is easier to just keep on keeping on doing stuff a certain way without energy-sapping re-examination. Thus the potential for self-deception grows exponentially over time.

It is easy to see these effects at work in the plight of 'Name Withheld.' She has embarked on a habit of 'going it alone,' what we might call the myth of self-sufficiency. She has sought 'success' as a one woman project, apparently with few or no mentors, friends or family relationships.

The greater her career independence and positive feedback, the easier it apparently became to believe in her own control. Such illusions encourage confusion between what you can control and those things beyond your control (fate, accident, chance, whatever term you prefer). When events beyond control occur, whether good or bad, victims of this form of self-deception often take credit for the good, and blame the bad on someone or something else. They can quickly develop a victim mentality. In 'Name's case, she sees herself as a victim of her own shortcomings.

Reliance on (unrealistic) expectations is another difficult habit to break. Optimism is a positive, even essential, characteristic of a potential loving partner. But the habit of relying on our expectations to judge reality leads easily to self-deception. The more convinced we are that we 'know' how things should be, the less likely we are to make good judgments. When we develop a very strong preconception of what our ideal 'soul' mate will look like, act like, or think like, we risk missing the real thing. Remember how disappointed the Jewish leaders were with Jesus?

Talk about failure to meet expectations! Our personal experience with expectations is hardly so traumatic, but it's a story worth telling and it's coming up soon.

C.S. Lewis illustrates another subtle, but destructive habit in *The Screwtape Letters*. Screwtape proudly describes one of his most satisfying triumphs in producing self-deception. His victim is the mother of Wormwood's patient. This middle-aged Englishwoman is clearly a less than ideal presence in the life of her son, who is most anxious to escape his childhood bedroom and extended childhood with mom. Screwtape exults at his success in turning this woman into a glutton! How can this be, given that she is abstemious to a fault, refusing all offerings at teatime with a flourish and requesting only plain tea with just a few drops of cream and a half teaspoonful of sugar? Screwtape explains patiently that the mother, in her elaborate refusal to enjoy 'teatime' offerings and in her precise demands about her plain tea is, in fact, indulging herself around her eating habits as surely as any glutton. She has made herself, and her food, the center of attention for all concerned, while believing, apparently sincerely, that she is both abstaining from full engagement with food *and* not causing anyone any trouble. Screwtape could not be prouder of his perverse success. Do you have any reaction to this story?? Ever encounter anything like this?

By way of contrast, Claire points out the story told of the sainted Therese of Lisieux, whose laser-like focus on her own mental habits is both commendable and a bit terrifying. No devil would seem to have a chance dealing with this nineteenth-century Frenchwoman. Therese refused to watch the birds she regularly fed enjoying their crumbs. She feared falling prey to feeling prideful about caring for God's creatures and thus abstained from ever witnessing the outcome of her loving, caring deeds! Now there, let's admit, is some serious focus on avoiding self-deception!

In fact, these two brief vignettes get to the essence of our concern with self-deception. It is all too easy to develop the habit of making your 'self' the major part of every decision. Perhaps without realizing it, you may think in transactional terms. "I do 'x' and s/he does 'y.'" It is easy to end up looking for fairness and keeping a scorecard. On the one hand, it is certainly important to value your self and to protect it from abuse or neglect. On the other hand, when concern for your self dominates all decision-making (and particularly when it is unconscious), it affects relations with other people. A loving relationship is not like buying a new car and using it as long as it works just as expected. You have gotten a 'good deal' only if you are getting your 'money's worth,' and so on and so on.

Because habits are so powerful, a discussion of self-deception must point out the importance of psychological flexibility. We all must cultivate the ability to apply our self-awareness, and to reset our behavior/attitudes as necessary as circumstances change. This is the work of building a loving and loveable self. As will become evident, it is also a fundamental skill in the creation of a long-term loving relationship with another human being.

At first glance, taking a pause to reset is an entirely practical strategy. It can and should be deployed for basic decision-making, whether to manage one's 'impulse' shopping proclivities or to review the investments in your retirement account. These 'pauses' may not offer glimpses into the transcendent, but they are essential for good decision-making when many factors are in play. An organizational leadership guru, Dov Seidman, has an excellent analogy for thinking about what happens in such moments.[13] It's a sports analogy, but stick with us. He talks about

---

[13] See Dov Seidman, *How: Why How We Do Anything Means Everything* (2007). More detail about pivots is found in our chapter on Imagination.

'pivots.' In basketball. the pivot position is usually occupied by the tallest team member, positioned under the basket looking out at teammates on the court. He/she is positioned to receive a pass and turn quickly, either right or left, to get off a short shot. In the maneuver, the pivot player plants one foot firmly (the pivot foot) and steps with the other to the side or directly toward the basket, shielding the ball from the defender. Seidman argues that leaders must constantly adjust to new information or changing conditions in a search for new opportunities. They too must pivot decisively. He calls the pivot foot that does not move the 'anchor,' based in the organization's permanent values and mission, while the other foot strikes a new direction/strategy/initiative. As long as the pivot foot does not move, the player can try new directions with the other foot multiple times. In basketball and in life, you must make new moves over and over again as conditions warrant. But it is a bad idea to move both feet at once! Without a pivot foot planted in core values, Name Withheld is blown about on the open seas, three sheets to the wind, as the old saying goes. Her agency has been lost.

As you may guess, this idea of core values is a very important 'anchor' in a long-term loving relationship. When the values are shared with another person, there is an anchor for whatever storm blows in. These values support your individual and collective agency. The energy required to carry out a reset or pivot is enabled by your agency. Each individual must bring an initial set of values to the party and building the self involves searching and testing these important concerns as an individual. It is easy to see manifestations of this search among young people who are easily influenced by peer pressures and the latest 'group think' fad. This is hard work and requires multiple resets during and after adolescence. But core values are so essential that such efforts should be sustained despite the cost in psychic energy and time.

Two quick observations are in order. First, trusted friends, relatives and 'experts' of various stripes can provide a valuable mirror to an individual by reflecting back ways in which his or her behavior impacts others. One should always be eager for such feedback and advice from someone whose judgment (and motives) you trust. You are, however, still obliged to use your conscience to judge whether the outside advice aligns with your personal values. You cannot outsource the responsibility for using your gift of self-consciousness (along with your built-in conscience) to assess and alter your own behavior/progress. Those who entrust such important decisions to a coach, a guru, a minister, a friend or a therapist are not building a self that they will be happy to live with, and worse, they will not possess a robust self to bring to a partnership with someone they love.

Secondly, self-examination and the process of resets should be repeated frequently.[14] Such rituals, in and of themselves, are neither positive or negative forces in a search for your best self. But they can serve an important purpose especially as your own core values become clearer. Resets should not produce fear of change or vulnerability, but rather renewed energy and a sense of optimism about the future. Confidence in your judgment when coping with change will add great value to any long term partnership.

Being engaged by 'the enduring,' if not 'the eternal,' while simultaneously living with the constant need for resets and pivots, is not an automatic conflict or source of tension. It is a unique

---

[14] The 'wisdom tradition' of the Catholic Church includes the sacrament of reconciliation (confession, in the old days), which embodies the combination of self-examination and reset. See Claire's discussion of her use of this practice in the next chapter. For some non-religious reset strategies, see Jancee Dunn, "7 Ways to Reset your Relationship," in the "Well" section of the *New York Times*, June 16, 2021. Dunn culls the research literature for practical ideas in a user-friendly format.

human capability that deserves each individual's appreciation and care. It is a manifestation of your material, ever-changing self, operating in time, co-existing with your spiritual self. When nurtured and strengthened, this spiritual self is not subject to the ravages of time. It is the 'you' that will form an immutable core of values throughout your life no matter your chronological age. Self-examination is the food for our spirits as surely as our lunch or dinner feeds our physical selves.

CHAPTER FOUR

The Odd Couple

As you can see, we have described a spectrum of self-understanding, ranging from total delusion to profound self-comprehension. You might consider St. Therese and the clueless mother of Wormwood's patient as the opposite ends of this spectrum. The great majority of us fall somewhere in the middle, with our share of blind spots and occasional perceptive insights about our own behaviors. We naturally invite you to think about this important dimension of your own character, and whether or how your place on the spectrum has changed over time.

So where did each of us, Claire and David, stand on this metric when we met? We promise to make this quick, but we found it revealing to look back through this lens at our own younger selves. Let's start with Claire, who was, shall we say, remarkably adept at wielding her free will, conscience and consciousness as a spiritually precocious teenager. She tells it this way:

> At thirteen, I was studying for Confirmation, the Catholic sacrament that prepares boys and girls for commitment to their faith. Sister Ann Regis cheerfully explained that God had given all of

us the gift of free will. We were responsible to choose right from wrong on our own. No one was making big decisions for us. She also taught us about 'sin,' the idea that humans could and did choose to disobey God's laws, like that story of Adam and Eve.

This all seemed pretty far-fetched to me. The idea of disobeying orders had never crossed my mind. In my house, the consequences of such behavior were too terrifying to even consider. It sounded plausible in the abstract, this 'free will' stuff, but sin was not on my agenda.

I now realize that, given her students' vulnerable age, Sister may have felt she needed to stress the temptations to sin that surrounded us. But I got a somewhat different message. I remember thinking that if sin is a choice of a person's will, only God (and I) could *really* know whether I was (hypothetically, of course) intentionally choosing to do the wrong thing.

I understood that using my free will to break a specific law of God, like "Thou shall not kill," could look like a sin to someone else. But, what if it was killing to defend someone else who couldn't defend herself, or in self-defense? Hurting someone else's feelings and causing them pain, on purpose? Sure. That would be me using my free will to do the wrong thing. That would break God's law to love one another. If I chose that, I chose to sin, like Adam and Eve did.

I decided to ask one of our more patient parish priests to meet with me and answer the big question: "Father, isn't it right that if sin is an act of a person's free will, then no one can tell you that you sinned. No one *but God and yourself*, not a priest or even a bishop or a Pope, right, Father?" After hours of discussion with yours truly, the budding theologian, Father Quentin Duncan, said yes, I was right. Sin must be the result of full consent of a person's free will to split from God. Father Duncan also advised me that the right pathway to making intelligent decisions using my free would require effort to understand the 'wisdom traditions' of the Church. I remember he said I was doing exactly the right thing by getting advice and thinking and even arguing my point of view. I wasn't going off and making my own rules. But yes, sin is the willful offense against God with thoughtful pre-consideration.

Little did I know that, through this process, I was learning to understand my own power to operate as a force in my own life… to be in control of my personal self, and potentially, other parts of life around me.

Claire is the first to admit that her experiences and behavior as a child and an adolescent were hardly typical, even back in the 1950s and '60s. Claire was the oldest of six children and the product of Catholic schools from kindergarten through high school. Her mother, still going strong at 99, was a homemaker and devout practitioner of her Catholic faith. Her father graduated from West Point as World War II neared its conclusion, and he was immediately trained as a fighter pilot and sent to the Pacific theater just after Claire's birth. There he was shot down and captured by the Japanese army, spending close to one year in prison. He survived and eventually returned to civilian life as a finance executive, first in the aeronautical industry and later in consumer electronics and fathered five siblings for Claire. But he never completely recovered from the trauma of his imprisonment, and his volatile personality made daily life an unpredictable and sometimes frightening experience for his family.

Childhood was not a carefree time for his eldest daughter, who inherited grown-up responsibilities for the care of her numerous younger siblings at a very early age. School was in fact something of a refuge and Claire spent recess time in the chapel at her elementary school where she 'met' St. Therese for the first time. The 'all-stars' of her faith, she learned from reading their stories, personified courage, flexibility, and a sense of purpose that provided inspiration to a little girl facing an endlessly challenging world. They became the 'friends' that her circumstances prevented her from developing in the 'real' world. And exemplary friends they were. There was St. Frances (Mother) Cabrini, who dreamed of going to China as a missionary, but was sent instead to New York City in the 1880s. The religious order she founded educated thousands of Italian immigrants, and a century later opened one of the first HIV-AIDS clinics in the Big Apple. There was St. Ignatius Loyola, the wealthy knight wounded in battle in 1520, who founded the Society of Jesus that created Jesuit institutions of higher education around the world. And Claire met St. Catherine of Siena, a fourteenth-century woman of little formal education whose spiritual and intellectual powers were so great that she eventually advised popes and politicians and reunified a divided church, becoming the patroness of Italy and a formal 'doctor of the Church' (in recognition of the profundity of her spiritual writings, an honor also accorded St. Therese of Lisieux). How could Claire go wrong with friends like these to inspire and guide her?

High school was dominated by two powerful authorities—her Dad and the cloistered nuns who taught at Holy Angels Academy. Their messages were identical: "You have nothing, *nothing* in common with boys your age." The nuns' message was framed more constructively, as in "we need all our own time to develop our lives as women." Claire was all in favor of developing her life as a woman, so she did not date in high school, nor, for that matter, during college either. After attending a couple of "mixers," she concluded that both Dad and the beloved sisters were, indeed, totally correct.

There was more than enough shocking behavior among her new female classmates at college, her first experience at a secular institution, specifically Connecticut College for Women. The girls regularly shimmied out of required chapel service by stretching out on the floor under their pews, carefully turning their heads to the entry door, and sliding till they reached the row nearest the door. Claire reacted with admiration, horror, and dismay:

> I had never even thought of breaking out of required anything, never mind *Chapel!!!* My secret admiration for their courage mingled with my ever deeper sense that these were not "my people."

As might be expected, Claire sought out a more familiar framework as she adjusted to a large dose of secular life amid peers with whom she had effectively no shared experiences. She signed up for a weekend retreat through the chaplain's office on campus where she met Sister Jane Symington, who became a trusted friend and guide throughout Claire's college experience:

Through many conversations over my four years of 'retreating,' she helped me explore what made me happy. What did I fear and why? What had I learned from watching my parents, my siblings, my college friends and teachers? What to avoid and what to step toward? She enabled me to imagine the life I could create in the future. She loved to tell me about the lives of the saints... how they faced difficulties, challenges, problems, confusions, mistakes and joys, successes, and how their confidence in God and their communication with Him helped them maintain joy as they pursued their life missions.

She also strengthened my commitment to the ritual of 'examination of conscience' and to the Sacrament of Reconciliation. I learned to spend time each week identifying my progress and failures in my effort to become the best version of myself. That's how I find my faults, my impatience, my sometimes excessive talking that drowns out the ideas of others. The list goes on. My goal is to live better for others and strive beyond day to day expectations. I can't do this alone, and I don't have to.

Reconciliation enables me to enter a thoughtful connection with my own spirit, with another person (the priest), and with the God Who Loves Me. I share the results of my self-examination with the two others present and 'confess' my shortcomings. I ask for God's forgiveness and promise to try to do better. My agency at work. In turn, I am 'forgiven' on the spot, absolved, and my mistakes disappear from God's memory. I 'go in peace.' There is no victimhood. Only optimism and a sense of my power to do better in the future.

Such powerful agency enabled Claire's deep sense of purpose. She felt called to help and protect others: her mother, her siblings, her college classmates. Moreover, given her hands-on childhood of caregiving, she could problem-solve in the real world, whether caring for children, counseling distressed roommates, or launching a profitable campus travel business to earn money to supplement her scholarship. Her investments in her spiritual self through the traditions of her Catholicism, including examination of conscience, prayer and the ritual of reconciliation, established an unshakable set of core values.

Claire's experience in the 'real' world, on the other hand, was clearly limited. She harbored some, shall we say, naïve expectations about how life might work in a larger framework. Her powerful agency had yet to be tested outside her large, traditional, Italian-American, Catholic family and her life as an (admittedly) untraditional college student in the 1960s. Graduate school would be a new environment of independence: earning a stipend, living on her own and pursuing a career, an uncharted pathway for a woman in Claire's powerful family culture. She prepared for this new life as a PhD student in French and Italian by heading to Europe the summer of her college graduation, alone, with $200 and the promise of some babysitting for a French family. She hitchhiked (alone) from Paris to the Amalfi Coast of Italy to visit relatives she had only heard about in family stories, and lived to tell about her adventures. She felt she was ready to handle anything that Indiana University in Bloomington, Indiana had to offer. Would her pivot foot stay anchored while she tested so many possible new directions? Did she even imagine what new moves to the basket she would need to create? To be continued…

David did not have the benefit of a running start when it came to preparing for a 'purpose-driven life.' He didn't spend much, if any, time worrying about whether he might be kidding himself about how the future might play out. In fact, he didn't worry much about the future at all as he headed to Indiana University for his PhD studies. He was mostly grateful to have avoided conscription in the military upon his college graduation. Self-examination was not his strong suit.

> I had lived a highly protected, only-child upbringing by two devoted parents. I was never called up to focus on needs other than my own. My parents, both from fragile economic backgrounds, had survived the Great Depression as newlyweds by living in my mother's childhood home, as they could not afford a place of their own. Eventually, they had realized the dream of buying a house in a modest suburb (50 x 110-foot lot, five-room bungalow in a Detroit suburb), where they lived for the rest of their lives. They continued to live with the constant awareness of the fragility of life in general. (My idea of running a household, as my parents did, by placing the monthly budgeted cash for food, gas, utilities, etc. in envelopes in a dresser drawer, did not prove effective over time.)
>
> There were no summer camps or tennis lessons in my growing up, but there was stability and, from my highly protected perspective, total security. My folks sacrificed to enable me to focus on school, sports and my interest in music. My community

provided good schools, good neighbors, and an overall sense of well-being. I worked, of course, because money mattered, from paper routes to lawn cutting, and eventually to land surveying each summer during high school and university (and even some side gigs in graduate school!). I also worked as a church organist throughout high school. I thus developed a sense of personal responsibility, but 'purpose' or even 'ambition' for me revolved around earning enough money to meet basic necessities, rather than worrying about the needs of others.

Obedience to rules framed the demands of home life. My parents were disciplined, religious, teetotaling people. My paternal grandfather was a Baptist minister (playing cards were the tickets of the devil, which may explain my love of card games!). My mother was a lifelong Sunday School teacher and her values were not up for discussion or debate in the household. These were givens. Ideas, in general, were not discussed or debated. When Little League baseball coaches (and local Boy Scout troop leaders) were seen drinking a can of beer, my scouting and baseball career came to a quick end. In retrospect, many of these folks were Catholics, which apparently contributed to my parents' discomfort with my participation (although the connection of alcohol and Catholicism, if any, was never discussed). Holidays were celebrated with like-thinking relatives, aunts and uncles but few cousins, and the high point of each summer was a two week family camping trip to northern Michigan.

Meanwhile, I moved on to high school. I was, on the surface, a clean cut straight-arrow, as they used to say, in a vaguely *American Graffiti* setting, although I wasn't above learning to smoke and shoplift with my friends. Drinking, on the other hand, was too aberrant for me to consider. High school proved an eye-opener, as a new cohort of students from a neighboring suburb joined the familiar group of all-White, all-Christian kids who had attended kindergarten, elementary, and junior high together (no one ever seemed to come or go from the community). The newcomers were generally more prosperous (some even had cars of their own!) and academically talented (or they worked harder—it was difficult to tell), and quite a few were Jewish! My enthusiasm for such gifted, vivacious female classmates (beauty *and* brains!) was met with coolness on the home front, so I was obliged to break the home rules and lie about it, in order to pursue my enthusiasms.

Then there was college and despite their dreams that I attend the small Presbyterian liberal arts school only a hundred miles down the road, my parents (who had not attended college) accepted my completely idiosyncratic idea to apply to Princeton University in some state on the East Coast that I had never visited. When a generous scholarship offer accompanied the admit letter, off I went without a clue, a friend, or a reference. My long-suffering mother not only had to deliver me to an empty room in need of (used) furniture to furnish it (shared with three other 'sophisticates' from New York City, New Orleans, and Seattle as roommates), but she set about making curtains for the room as only a mother would.

Little of this seemed like the remarkable privilege it was to an 18 year old whose world travels at the time were limited to Upper Michigan camping sites and a 'cruise' to Buffalo, NY through the Great Lakes. Among my gifted and experienced Princeton peers, I focused, not surprisingly, on my own survival. I had not been tested by any serious challenges in my life up to this point, unlike the many challenges Claire faced on a daily basis. My response was less than heroic, but it did enable me to carry on with modest success. My reset enabled me to make the most of this unlikely opportunity as the first in my family to attend college.

I adjusted to life in the 'middle of the pack' as a competent but unexceptional midwestern, public school scholarship boy in the Ivy League. I bussed tables in the dining hall as part of my scholarship requirement. My music skills failed to impress the University organist (who was, after all, a world class player). My Presbyterian sense of rhythm prevented me from success as a keyboardist in any of the campus rock bands. Typically (and mercifully in retrospect), there was no "dark night of the soul" as these realizations took root. I was anxious but never threatened. I adopted the path of least resistance in most important decisions like choosing a major with little attention to core principles or big ideas or personal aspirations. This approach, in retrospect, caused me to miss a variety of opportunities that might have led me into different fields of endeavor, but I chose Romance Languages "cuz I liked to read novels and I could already do that in English" and had my only decent grades in introductory literature courses.

Upon graduation, it seems fair to say, my investments in my core values were still limited. My conscience was fluid at best. I had acquired an unattractive habit over my teen years of deceiving my parents rather than confronting them when potential disagreements arose. Conflict was onerous and to be avoided. I had faced the challenge of the East Coast Ivy League 'pivot' from a midwestern high school and survived, but I had not broken any new ground with creative moves to the basket.

On the other hand, I had gained some measure of self-awareness. I was certainly aware of my limitations. Any misguided or unrealistic expectations had been quickly squashed. I was responsible, self-reliant and reasonably even-tempered. I could and did live with the consequences of my actions. My sense of humor and love of music, both pop and classical, had been sustained and refined at college. I was open-minded and not given to judging other people. I did not feel arrogant, given my modest achievements at Princeton. Was I self-deceived? Or self-aware? Like most people, it was probably a mix of the two. In retrospect, I certainly failed to grasp the enormity of the security and privilege I had enjoyed up to this point in my life. By the time I met Claire, I had traveled and worked in England and France. I felt reasonably comfortable and presentable in a variety of settings— geographic, religious, familial, intellectual, wealthy and working class. I was competent at auto repair, land surveying, bridge, golf, fishing, poker, rock and roll trivia, ice hockey, and the French language, and had written a well-received thesis on existentialism. What more could any girl want?

As we wrap up Part One, let's remind ourselves about the big ideas at play. Everyone, when entering into 'coupledom' with another person, brings a back story with them. It would be foolish to try to generalize about a specific set of steps or actions that would ensure long term success for every set of new partners. What we do want to emphasize is the importance of using each partner's gifts of free will, self-awareness and a conscience to fight the plague of self-deception.

This devilish curse, as C.S. Lewis illustrates, can undercut the most well-intentioned actions. It is *the* enemy of a long-term, loving relationship. This might be a moment to re-read Name Withheld's letter to remind yourself of the damage—the loss of your agency—that can occur without regular attention to reflection, resets and reboots.

When two people do decide to commit to a shared life, these issues remain important, needless to say. But now it becomes more important to think of free will, consciousness and conscience as shared assets and the work of fending off 'self-deception' as a shared project. Such a big idea cannot be taken on casually. It is not a contractual arrangement. Your entire self—body, mind and spirit—is about to become indivisible from your partner's—a shared agency, assuming you are serious about the quest for real love.

So let's start thinking about coupledom and some of the ways of living that can contribute to the creation of a shared self.

PART TWO

Coupledom

CHAPTER FIVE

The Search For A Better Half

Take a look back at those mournful words from the song "Lookin' for Love" quoted in our Introduction. They sound almost quaint today, as the 'search for love' is more likely to occur online than in beer-soaked singles bars. But whether online, at work, at school, or in a bar, the search is still propped up by dreams of a magical connection to an as yet unknown perfect mate. Over two thousand years ago, Plato spoke in terms of finding one's alter ego, of uniting with the missing half of your essential self. As the song suggests, a great deal of time and effort may well be spent kissing frogs in search of Prince (or Princess) Charming.

We have a search story from back in the dark ages of the early twentieth century, handed down through Claire's family. It serves as an excellent introduction to the coupling process, at a time when this undertaking was, shall we say, a bit more structured than today:

> Dinner was served. The unsuspecting young suitor sat at the family table on a first 'date' with my grandmother (nonna Rosa) in Italy in 1902. Little did he know that my great grandmother's

(bis-nonna's) ingenious Suitor Sorting Machine was humming quietly along. He approached the moment of truth as he finished his salad course. Bis-nonna announced that her daughter had personally baked the dessert to please her guest and asked Rosa to bring the confection to the table. No Olympic judge was ever more tough-minded than this dear lady. And why not? The happiness of her eldest daughter was at stake.

Rosa returned to the table with a perfectly prepared and decorated tiramisu. She placed it in front of her mother who cut the portions. She passed the first to the head of the house, her husband, the second to Rosa's suitor, and then to the rest of the table.

The suitor's test was *on*. He had only seconds to succeed or fail forever. Some of the candidate bachelors who had visited over the years had no particular reaction to a special dessert made just for them. Nonplussed, they were used to fine things, to efforts made to please them. This moment was just another of them. These guys were toast! Immediately Doomed. Out. "Nonplussed" does not a great husband make.

Another suitor had been studied and cool—reserved. He played to the alpha male at the head of the table. With a silent approving nod and smile after the first bite, he resumed discussion of the size of the grape harvest that year, given the amount of rain and sun. Likewise—the sophisticate's goose was cooked—forever. If he could ignore his potential sweetheart after she had clearly *not* ignored him, he was not a passable husband prospect—no sense wasting time on him.

"Women in our family know how to make a man happy in a thousand ways," Bis-nonna would whisper to her often-disappointed daughter. "They should only marry men who know how to express rich gratitude with enthusiasm! How will his appreciation sound after ten, twenty or forty years of marriage, if it is dull as a suitor???" Rosa's mother waited through each test, adamant that she would not surrender her eldest daughter to any man who could not demonstrate genuine gratitude for the gifted ministrations of a woman he would wish to marry.

Claire was told this story countless times by her aunts, her mother and her own nonna (that would be Rosa). To a little girl, the story seemed romantic. Later, it seemed quaint. And eventually kind of silly. All those dinners. All that waiting and all those disappointments. We will get to the end of the story later on, but of course Nonna did find a suitable suitor (or Claire wouldn't be here!). She was, however, obliged to wait until age 26, right on the verge of spinsterhood in those days!

So why start with this old fashioned story? Because it tees up the fundamentals of so-called 'real love.' Bis-nonna understood that love could grow only if one party actively admired and respected the other (and these sentiments were returned in equal measure). Despite the preoccupation with money and status that the story suggests, she insisted that mutual appreciation was *the* essential factor for a couple's long-term happiness. Her daughter would not be 'given away' to a man who did not both appreciate the gift he was receiving *and* express his gratitude for it (her).

Such calculated intervention in the search process was clearly designed to counterbalance the emotionally-charged experience of 'falling in love.' How could an inexperienced young person know what to look for in a potential mate? Surely the experienced adults were more knowledgeable about such things and it would be irresponsible not to put this knowledge to work in the search process.

Fast forward fifty years or so and we find a different kind of story about lookin' for love, this one told by C.S. Lewis. In *The Screwtape Letters*, you recall, the young 'patient' is in search of a suitable partner, and in his case, his mother seems singularly missing in action (and no father is ever mentioned). Instead we get a running commentary on his struggles from the devils whose intent is to subvert any opportunity for happiness that may come his way. In the process, we get a play-by-play of the pitfalls of the coupling process.

Let's start with what the devils call 'falling in love' to distinguish the condition from 'real love.' Screwtape points out the crazy, often irresponsible things that humans excuse by saying simply that they have 'fallen in love.' Of course, what they mean is that they are currently under the influence of a flood of strong hormones operating primarily to ensure the continued reproduction of the species, rather than the transcendent or spiritual joys of shared selfhood over a lifetime. Under such conditions, an experienced devil will sense an opportunity to leverage self-deception and perhaps cause real harm to the physical, mental and spiritual well-being of the individuals involved. Unrealistic expectations about the new found love interest are but one of many ways that these devious foes of human happiness can poison the building process of a loving relationship at the outset.

But 'falling in love' is part of the deal. Of course this phase is risky. Imagine finding oneself overtaken by constant thoughts of another person and an overwhelming desire to be close in body, mind and spirit. There is no avoiding risk in the coupling process and some of that libidinal energy can enable two people to overcome daunting barriers to creating a union. But some self-awareness in the midst of these emotions is critical. Perhaps there is a way to spare you our own story of 'falling in love,' but no! You knew you would eventually hear the story of how we met, the beginning of our coupledom. It's a perfect illustration of the expectations we all develop about our futures and inevitably, about the partner we imagine sharing that future. Given Claire's strong personal sense of purpose, her expectations were particularly high:

> In September, 1968, I arrived in Bloomington, Indiana, to pursue my PhD in French Literature. With two hundred dollars in a new checking account, I would be supporting myself on my tiny Teaching Assistant monthly check. I expected to finish at Indiana University as quickly as possible and to begin a career as a professor of French literature and language.
>
> The Midwest was a new world for an Italian-American Catholic Jersey girl. I learned that olive oil was sold only in the local pharmacy as an emetic! My rented room in town came with kitchen privileges (and one shelf) for 15 minutes each evening, overseen by my landlady, Eunice,

who had just purchased the house after spending her life on a nearby farm.

Shortly after classes began, I came home to disaster! Eunice was at the door of the house, arms folded firmly across her very ample chest. She looked fierce. She screamed at me... "I will *not* have it in *my home*, young lady. Get all your things out of my house immediately! Right after you get that wine out of my kitchen, out of my house and poured into the sewer down the block... not into my sewer. I will not have it. What kind of a woman do you think I am?? Rules are rules. I told you when I let you move in, *no drinking, no alcohol, in my house, ever!!!*"

I tried to explain that the bottle was not wine. It was vinegar, for salads. Impossible to drink. To no avail. As Eunice became increasingly angry, I fled to the kitchen, emptied the little bottle into a nearby sewer, and packed my room in tears. I called a cab to take my boxes, luggage, lamps and books to the Holiday Inn, glad that my credit card would save me for the night.

The next morning, the IU student housing office was my first stop. They had no apartments or dorm rooms available at this late date, but lucky for me they had a two-story house near campus, empty because a visiting faculty member had failed to get his visa in time for this semester. Of course, I couldn't afford the monthly rent alone. I pulled out my burdened credit card and dragged my stuff to 409 Highland Avenue. Within the week, I had located two female co-renters. But this was not the launch to my graduate studies that I had envisioned.

Meanwhile, on the academic side, I had attended my first graduate class, on the modern French essay, with a famous professor. As I entered our classroom, I looked across toward the windows. Click. I still see the snapshot from 56 years ago! Leaning forward, his right elbow on the desk's writing tablet, hand under his chin, yellow pencil held by his right ear. Nice profile, dark curly hair, blue oxford button down shirt with sleeves folded back a few times, khaki slacks, was David Graham Burnett.

What? Why? Well, I made sure we talked at the break. We set up time to share a coffee and our Gauloise smokes (essential for all francophiles). Soon afterwards, David invited me to see a movie with him. I accepted despite potentially breaking my PhD rule: no dates for the first three years... *no distractions.* I reasoned that he was just trying to be nice to me. Decent excuse, I thought... Memorable evening... at the movies, *Alphaville,* which had been shot at the Exxon building in Paris where David had worked the previous summer.

I was nervous letting David bring me to my new empty house after our movie. So, I decided to invite him to have dinner together at the house on Highland the next evening. I could tell him that at the front door without letting him in. I remembered my commitment to myself. Men *after* the doctoral coursework was done, not before.

Truth be told, I found myself quite taken by this David. In just a month of knowing him, I felt a weird buzz, a happy, but, for me, weird feeling around him. I remember saying a prayer that I could stay focused on my goals and see how to reject potential distractions. Happily I soon received divine guidance.

David had graciously volunteered to do the shopping for the planned dinner at my house, and my credit card definitely needed the help. As he unpacked the Kroger bags (whatever Kroger was??), I saw a box of Velveeta (a cheese product?), a bag of Tiptop white bread, a large round iceberg lettuce, a can of green beans, and a bottle of salad dressing, Russian, as I remember. In all my years (23 by then), none of these items had ever been in a kitchen with me. If this is what David Graham Burnett considered food, God had made clear that I didn't have to worry about being tempted to kiss him, fall in love with him, or ruin my career goals. I remember feeling some regret, but also relief.

We won't force you to labor through the rest of our first year of graduate school. But we were engaged to be married by the following June and David never ate iceberg lettuce again (nor bottled salad dressing). We both pivoted in short order from very different independent expectations to the dream of a shared life. As it happened, when Claire broke the happy news to her mother,

Mom responded with some news of her own. She was expecting! Speaking of expectations...

Thus began our first exposure as a couple to the vagaries that fate has in store. Claire dropped out of grad school to return home to assist her mother with this very belated pregnancy. She taught high school French and our love affair became a commuter relationship. We adjusted, not without difficulty, and forged ahead with wedding plans for the following June when Claire's new baby brother would be a few months old.

The wedding was a classic, happy affair with large turnouts from both families despite what must have been grave misgivings on both sides. People kept their worries to themselves and the new couple headed to the airport for the aforementioned three months of honeymooning travel across Europe. Then it was back to Bloomington and a basement apartment using David's college bunk beds (side by side) in our 'master' bedroom.

So enough for the moment with the diary entries and let's focus on what had just occurred, i.e. the launching of a shared life through the ritual of marriage. The embrace of marriage is considerably less common today than it was fifty-odd years ago for a wide variety of reasons, social, religious, and economic. But marriage has never lost its popularity entirely and we want to reflect a bit up front on the importance of this 'launching pad' toward a lifetime commitment. Certainly every serious couple faces the big question at some point: should we/will we get *married*?

CHAPTER SIX

Marriage And Habits That Matter

"Marriage is a conversation," or so said the German philosopher Friedrich Nietzsche. The marriage question is essential, in our mind, because it introduces the fundamental distinction between actions we have dubbed 'transactional' and those we are calling 'transcendent.' Remember that transcendence invokes the spiritual dimension of the self and opportunities for experience of a type that cannot be explained in purely rational or physical terms.

There is always a transactional dimension to marriage, by which we mean the choice of formalizing the coupling through a public ceremony that includes witnesses to an exchange of vows or promises between members of the couple. These vows, in turn, are recorded with the 'state' in virtually all societies. Society at large has always had an interest in knowing who belongs to what family, who the parents of children are and therefore who is responsible for their care and well-being. There are obvious economic dimensions to this decision as well, as the treatment of income for tax purposes is defined by marriage status. So too is the inheritance of assets, obligations for child support and alimony in case the marriage is legally dissolved, and so on.

At various points in history, marriage was predominantly transactional in nature, often arranged by parties other than the individuals being married, such as parents or relatives. There were contracts galore to define the nature and size of the dowry that the woman brought to the marriage and other details. Such 'arranged marriages,' even among two parties who have never met, are still common in some societies today. In so-called modern societies where independence and individualism reign, couples sometimes create their own 'prenuptial agreement' to define the terms of their commitment and a path forward, at least financially, in the event of divorce. Such is the power of transactions and the zero-sum world in which they operate. We should be clear. Transactions are essential and important aspects of life. There is nothing wrong, ethically or morally, with focusing on transactions in life and in relationships. Our concern is to point up the limitations of such an orientation when two people are striving to build a shared love.

Just as there are varying degrees of 'transactionality' in marriage, so too is there a continuum of transcendence. Every couple that freely chooses to formalize their bond through public vows presumably does so for at least some reasons that can be considered 'transcendent.' Partners may wish to convey their love publicly , and thus to bring pleasure and happiness to one another. Such generosity is a powerful motivator and difficult to explain in purely material terms. Offering a public vow of lifetime loyalty, obedience, and care in sickness and in health is the ultimate gift that one has to offer to another person. It is a pledge of the self, the initiation of the project through which two selves are merged into a single indivisible being.

All this can be done, and frequently is, in a civil setting without reference to, or engagement with, organized religion. We noted in our introduction that such engagement is not essential for the care of the human spirit, but billions of people the world over still continue to reach out for divine guidance, particularly at times of great importance in their lives. We will have more to say about such behavior in the coming chapters.

So weddings in religious settings continue in large numbers and various organized religions have their own rituals and practices to offer couples who wish to have their commitment to one another 'blessed' through the involvement of an ordained religious leader. When we consider the 'transcendent' dimension of marriage, the Catholic Church advances perhaps the most radical position. Here is (non-Catholic) David's understanding of the Catholic sacrament of marriage:

> Claire and I were married in a Catholic church ceremony (with a Protestant minister participating). I had no clear grasp at the time of the challenging framework we were operating in. I think I was pretty much on autopilot. Now I understand that the Catholic Church teaches that the vows exchanged by those who choose to wed in the Church are, in themselves, transformational. You are changed immediately and forever. Bingo! Persons completing the sacrament of marriage, repeating vows that date back hundreds of years, in front of 'vetted' witnesses, are transformed by the ritual. Each now exists as 'spouse' of his/her partner, a new state of being. Pledged permanently in mind, body and spirit. And this transformation, according to Church doctrine, is irreversible if entered into in good faith.
>
> I now see this bit of doctrine as an example of what Claire calls the 'wisdom tradition' of organized

religion. There is a lot of 'stuff' in organized religion—traditions, rituals, rules, judgments— that may seem out of touch in modern times. But there is accumulated wisdom as well, not to be discarded out of frustration, as Claire so wisely notes. Committing to an action that overtly invokes transcendence is a fitting way to embark on the journey to love.

This view of marriage is one hundred percent 'transcendent.' It is not a transaction in goods or services (or minds and bodies). It is spiritual transformation of both parties (when they are acting in good faith) and it cannot be undone by lawyers, no matter how skilled.

We admit that it is a lot to grasp, the idea of 'instant, permanent' transformation through words uttered. The Catholic Church, however, makes a clear point. Do not make these vows casually. Do not 'try it and see if you like it.' It is human nature to avoid risk, as we have discussed, and does it not make sense to 'hedge your bets' when it comes to marriage? I can always bail out if things go badly. (Guess the kids will work it out... maybe). Not according to the Church! These vows are high risk and high reward and there is *no* turning back if you wish to stay in good standing with the Church on earth. (It's harder to know what God thinks exactly about such institutional rules, but it's a safe bet that He is not pleased when people expressly vow to do something while invoking His name, and then say, "well, never mind.")

While few brides and grooms fully grasp, or even consider, an act of such radical transcendence, every couple contemplating marriage should engage this 'sacramental' dimension of their undertaking, with or without Catholicism. It is a cliché to note that every marriage will encounter difficulties and conflict along the way to real love, but it is in such difficult times that the radical commitment to one another serves its purpose.

Considering marriage in our discussion of coupledom is also essential, we believe, because, as noted in the Nietzsche quote, marriage is another word for 'conversation,' or dialogue, if you prefer. We like the idea of marriage as a conversation because it conveys the dynamic nature of creating a shared self with another person. It is an ongoing process to continue to learn about and with one's lifelong companion. Phrases such as 'being married' or 'in a marriage' focus on the static dimension. Marriage is indeed a 'state of being,' but our material selves are absolutely 'in time,' and a couple, married or otherwise, is at least partially in time as well, becoming together a living self. Think of marriage as both a noun (a state of being) and a verb (an action in time).

A conversation also implies ongoing engagement in a learning process with another person. It invokes both listening and speaking, sharing ideas and receiving reactions. It is hardly necessary to underscore how fundamental such interaction is to building a joyful partnership. A constructive conversation often includes questions, and the marriage vows are based on asking and answering potent questions. Do you take this man? Do you promise to? and so on.

But these questions are just the beginning of a lifetime of dialogue, because a shared self does not operate as two independent agents. Yes, agency is fundamental to the potential partner, but shared agency with a loving partner is just that, shared. There are no longer decisions taken separately, or actions without consideration of the other's wants and needs. That is a given in the building process.

The remainder of Part Two is given over to a discussion of what we are calling 'habits of mind' that couples can deploy regularly to enhance the chances of success of their own building process. We are positing that you have a genuine interest in creating and sustaining a monogamous, lifetime relationship with a loving partner. Of course, there is the challenge of finding a 'soul mate' willing to join you on the journey and take his or her responsibilities for the success of the project as seriously as you do. But there is no better way to sort out potential partners than to engage them in the above-mentioned 'conversations' about the ideas we are sharing. His or her willingness to think deeply about these matters, and to contribute to the couple's shared understanding, is a pretty good way to judge whether the odds favor a successful partnership.

When we asked ourselves which habits of mind have contributed the most to our joyfulness, we surprised even ourselves. Ready? The first recommendation is to cultivate your sense of humor! The second is to deepen and refine your practice of attention. And finally, we urge you to work on energizing and deploying your (shared) imagination. But quick, before you reject these items as just another set of bullet points on some slide, let us try to show you their practical value in building love that is more than a set of transactions.

Love can only flourish in an environment of trust, generosity and, dare we say it, beauty. These are 'transcendent' values well beyond the capacity of your instinctive, self-centered self. Practicing the habits of mind of humor, attention and imagination will keep the gator in his place away from the controls of your life. You and your partner will control the meaning and trajectory of your shared life, no matter what fate has in store. A shared investment in one another will produce a shared agency. Love requires two (authentic) agents to choose each other over and over and over.

There can be no outside forces calling the shots. It takes stamina and self-confidence to merge a well-developed self with a willing partner. That's why the personal agency we discussed in Part One is an essential building block for a long term success.

CHAPTER SEVEN

Humor

"Humor involves a sense of proportion and a
power of seeing oneself from the outside."
C.S. Lewis, *Preface to The
Screwtape Letters* (1961)

"A sense of humor frees us from vanity, on
the one hand, and from pessimism on the
other by keeping us greater than what we do,
and larger than what can happen to us."
Auguste Penjon[15]

Once you have engaged your will power, consciousness, and
conscience on your own behalf, you will naturally become a more
active problem solver. You are unlikely to simply drift along from
day to day as 'Name Withheld' clearly did. The more active you
are, however, the more potential there is to encounter resistance
and even conflict. Add in your (new) partner, and the probabilities
of friction increase exponentially. We think of humor as the ideal
'lubricant' for such friction in life. It will reduce wear and tear and
preserve your agency over time. And, just to be clear, we are using

---

[15] Quoted in John Morreall, *Comedy, Tragedy and Religion* (1999).

the term 'humor' to mean a sense of humor, an ability to identify and respond to various incongruities (including about yourself) with control and even appreciation.[16]

The ability to identify and create humor in your daily life is a great asset to well-being. It is guaranteed to make you more cheerful and optimistic. We recognize that this observation will not come as a great surprise. People who laugh readily, at themselves and the incongruities/ironies of life, generally attract others who are cheered by their company. When building a loving partnership over time, humor will greatly facilitate the process. The goal, as always, is to create a bond with your partner that transcends a mere 'working relationship.'

We have this information, by the way, on authority from Dame Folly herself. Thanks to her intermediary, Erasmus, the scholar who gave her voice in the sixteenth century,[17] she asserts that she holds the power to make interpersonal relationships possible. Only she can facilitate constructive human interactions. A totally rational relationship with oneself, or with a friend, partner or spouse, would, she argues, most likely end in despair if not suicide. We must ignore, or 'foolishly' set aside the failings of others in order to enjoy their company and to work effectively with them. All rational analysis would leave us no room to tolerate their shortcomings or individual idiosyncrasies. The same must be said,

---

[16] For a gently technical overview of the dynamics of humor from a neuroscience perspective, consider "Humor, Laughter, and Those Aha Moments" in *On The Brain: The Harvard Mahoney Neuroscience Institute Newsletter*, Vol 16, No.2, Spring 2010. The article helpfully distinguishes between humor (an evoked response from the brain, etc.) and laughter, which the author calls 'social signaling,' that is, a sign to other humans that the laughing person is not a danger (kinda depends, doesn't it?).
[17] Desiderius Erasmus, *In Praise of Folly*, 1511, or sometimes translated *The Praise of Folly*.

she notes, about ourselves. Ever know anyone who had difficulty tolerating him or herself? These are among the most difficult people to be around for any period of time.

> In sum [says Dame Folly], no society, no union in life, could be either pleasant or lasting without me. A people does not for long tolerate its prince, or a master tolerate his servant, a handmaiden her mistress, a teacher his student, a friend his friend, a wife her husband, a landlord his tenant, a partner his partner, or a boarder his fellow-boarder, except as they mutually or by turns are mistaken, on occasion flatter, on occasion wisely wink, and otherwise soothe themselves with the sweetness of folly.[18]

So there you have it. Humor is the launch pad for a journey to a generous, non-transactional life together. It will energize the practices of attention and imagination, and together these habits will build your spirit and your love with a partner!

A brief caveat is in order. Humor is a double-edged sword. It can cut and injure as surely as it can soothe and engender joyfulness. Humor can be weaponized. It is the bully's cruel and demeaning tool to diminish others. It can be perverted to deflect judgment. What about the serial unfaithful partner who draws attention to his or her failings in conversation? Or the miserly friend who makes a joke out of a well-known unwillingness to pay a fair share when the bill is presented? Such blatant attempts to diminish these shortcomings through joking reflect the devil's handiwork of self-deception in action.[19] Remember that your personal devil is never

---

[18] Quoted in John Morreall, *Taking Laughter Seriously* (1983), pp. 119–20.
[19] One can likewise see the devil's hand in humor that is used to disrespect another person indirectly. A 'flippant' attitude dismisses ideas that others

far away, and you cannot count on being assigned a rookie. You might, for instance, have to deal with a master like Screwtape on a daily basis. But enough with 'giving the devil his due.' Should you encounter or indeed produce such behaviors yourself, look over your shoulder quickly and maybe even mutter a sharp 'Begone!' Humor should serve to advance self-understanding, optimism, and just the right amount of humility.

What better way to think about humor than with a joke? Ready?

So a tourist stops a passerby on the sidewalk in Manhattan. "How do I get to Carnegie Hall?"

"Practice! Practice! Practice!" responds the New Yorker.

What on earth does such a corny ancient joke tell us about dealing with difficult marriage moments? "Gee, I'm glad you asked…" as the Borscht Belt comics used to say. For openers, the structure of this joke is typical of many language-based jokes. (This is the wonky part of the discussion. It's short!) The opening plays on the listener's habit of forming expectations as soon as incoming information is received. We 'know' what is coming next; at least our brain quickly arrives at a range of possible answers. But, oops! We are tricked by the response. Our expectation is revealed to be off track, although the punch line of the joke is entirely plausible, just unanticipated. In fact, the more sensible the punch line when the joke shifts registers, the funnier it often is.

---

offer. Such behavior implies that the topic has already been exhausted by those in the know. The flippant individual thus erects a wall of protection around him/herself and the closed world he or she inhabits. The other is diminished while the self is protected. Such subtle perversion of the power of humor contributes nothing to a respectful, let alone a transcendent, relationship with another person.

This kind of simple humor exploits our efficient, rational adult 'mind' and thus our penchant for predictability. At first we are surprised by the shift because we failed to calculate accurately 'what was coming.' We should appreciate that our expectations have been subverted and we are obliged, even fleetingly, to 'see' ourselves lose control of the narrative. We have to reset expectations. A refined sense of humor will cultivate an appreciation for the many ways that language (or many other circumstances) can shift us unexpectedly into a position requiring re-assessment of our own mental penchant for unconscious ways of thinking and doing. A joke of the type we are examining is humbling in a gentle, cheerful way. It reminds us that all of us are vulnerable to unanticipated (and unpredictable) events. Such experience, in turn, supports our agency, as we cope with the unexpected. We are not threatened, but rather bemused, by our vulnerability and thus better prepared for blows of fate of a more serious nature. A mini-lesson in self-awareness in twenty words or less. And self-awareness, we repeat, is an essential step toward eliminating or at least reducing self-deception.

We can't help but love this silly joke for another reason as well. The unexpected answer uses a key word in the cultivation of spirituality—practice. One does need to 'practice' a sense of humor to capture its benefits. As noted earlier, we all appreciate an individual who somehow has the ability to 'see' what is happening in a sufficiently objective way as to crack a joke when others are stressed. We bet you cannot keep from smiling at the story of the London shopkeeper who, during the nightly WWII bombing raids, dutifully kept a sign in his window that read "Open as usual." When the shop's windows were blown out one night, the next morning the sign read "More open than usual!" The degree of 'agency,' the control of the meaning of circumstance demonstrated by this affecting joke, makes one instinctively want to know the shopkeeper and hope for his/her company in difficult circumstances. Such control, such ability to direct the narrative of what is happening, rather than succumbing to the very understandable fear and anger of the 'blitz,' signals an individual with powerful agency, one who is well worth knowing and emulating. Putting humor into practice with a partner enables control of your shared mindset, no matter what chance (or perhaps the devil) throws your way.

We have a family moment that fits the bill. By now, you know that Claire is a serious person with remarkable agency and self-control. Everything about how she lives is oriented to loving and caring about others. A decade or so ago, she was stricken with a hemorrhagic stroke (brain bleed) and was hospitalized in a state of semi-consciousness for several days. Her doctors visited frequently, using a standard protocol to determine her level of awareness. What is your name? Where are you? Who is the president of the United States? What day is it? and so on. It took a few days, but one day, she had apparently had enough! "Why are you asking me these stupid questions?" she barked. "Let me ask you a few and see how smart you guys are. Do you know your ass from a hole in the ground?" Several equally challenging questions followed.

The doctors were delighted! This was good news, as Claire was able to speak for the first time. But the family team was taken aback. It was as though she had come back to life as her fighter pilot father! This new self picked up steam in the following days, as the nurses and orderlies, the cleaners and the food service folks smelled hell on an hourly basis for their failures and shortcomings. Our little family spent half the time apologizing on her behalf and the other half not knowing whether to laugh or cry.

Mercifully, thanks to the hospital's extraordinary care, she gained strength and was soon able to move to a rehab facility to begin the hard work of recovery. Her former self gradually re-emerged as well. However, let it be said that no one in the family has ever allowed her to forget (actually, she remembers nothing, of course) this episode. She is reminded at every opportunity that lurking inside her is "Big Daddy" (not a term of affection in our parlance) and we regularly quote her most vile reprimands from the hospital days as examples of her problem-solving skills. Does any of this matter? Well, it does to all of us who love her and can now manage the trauma of those days through lots of laughs. Happily, the family knows enough to avoid this kind of behavior where David is concerned. He overlooks Claire's insistence on referring to his fly fishing attire as "wearing rubber pants."

Cultivation of humor, in short, supports a flexible mindset that can absorb shocks that might damage more rigid thinking. If you can learn to 'take a joke,' that is, if you can overcome the momentary loss of dignity that may accompany being 'in the dark' about a joke, you are building flexibility, humility and your agency. A joke can puncture the veneer of competency and 'dignity' that all of us have a tendency to arm ourselves with. Children (and grandchildren), in our experience, offer endless opportunities to cast off the rigidities of adulthood in favor of reclaiming the 'silliness' (and endless creativity) of childhood. We always dressed up for Halloween with our children; we celebrated children's half birthdays (can't have too many birthdays when you're a kid), complete with half a birthday cake and 'Happy Birthday" sung with every other word. And lately, Claire's fully-recovered agency allows her a break from adulthood with her grandkids:

> One of my favorite routines is to invite my grandkids to do a "make-over" for me at my dressing table. I sit innocently while the giggling child, eyebrow pencil in hand, makes Groucho Marx eye brows and slowly draws in a beard and

mustache! A lipstick applied to the end of my nose and my hair combed into bizarre configuration adds peals of laughter from the child while I remain deadly serious and expectant.

I ask "How is it going? Is the whole family going to love how I look at dinner?" The child in charge of the presentation usually assures me that the make-over will make everyone so happy and I say many thank you's and suggest I will require a really special make-over to go to work next week, and perhaps the child would have some free time to re-do this great make-over! More peals of laughter... assurances of availability.

Imagine the child's leading me to the dinner table all "made over!" Total glee while the rest of the family raves and laughs... hugs and laughing all around... affirmation of how funny and fun I am... whole new kinds of dignity... never taking oneself too seriously, the joy of putting the youngest in charge!! Humor remains the real power and delight!!!

Self-confident people with well-developed agency don't mind being 'in the dark' for the time of the joke telling and are more often willing to laugh, to admit openly to being 'taken in' or tricked by the unexpected. Such folks probably enjoy the jokes even more because they are not threatened by a momentary condition of 'victimhood.'

The self-important, on the other hand, have forever been inviting targets for satiric humor. Satire plays on the lack of self-awareness of the self-important. Self-centered figures can be easily 'deflated' by pointing up their personal blindness. Thus humor of the satiric sort is an ideal weapon for the social critic and the free press. Self-important people, in our experience, almost always like to tell jokes, because, knowing the punchline, they feel a sense of empowerment over their listeners. We came across an historical example of an 'important person' who turned the tables on his 'important colleagues.' It clearly doesn't happen often but here is one of Claire's Catholic 'all-stars' (albeit an obscure one) in action.

Saint Philip Neri (1515–1590) earned his way to the hall of fame with (or in spite of?) his embrace of the ridiculous.[20] He seemed intent on entertaining God with his antics, but of course, he was doing his best to teach his fellow sinners on earth the value of humility and joyfulness. He defined humor as "a special kind of sense of proportion which is delighted rather than distressed by the inappropriateness in things." He had clearly mastered the difference between the comic imperfections of life on earth in comparison to the timeless perfection of the divine. He showed up at formal church events with half his beard shaven and one or more of his priestly vestments inside out, including his cardinal's hat, which he often wore backwards. Looking ridiculous and being laughed at was his way to insist on remaining humble (and perhaps flagging the important 'airs' of his fellow cardinals?).

Neri founded a 'congregation' of his followers dedicated to helping the poor in Rome and his reputation attracted many would-be adherents. But he insisted that there be no 'stuffed shirts' in his crew! On one occasion, a wealthy young Roman prince met with Neri to request admission to the Oratorians. Neri told the prince that he would have to pass a test. Philip produced a long foxtail and told the young man he should attach it to the back

---

[20] See V.J. Matthews, *St Philip Neri: Apostle of Rome and Founder of the Congregation of the Oratory*, 1934.

of his elegant frock coat and then walk quite gravely through all the streets of Rome for a day. Overwhelmed, the prince said he had come to Neri's congregation to win honor, not shame and embarrassment. Neri informed him that among the Oratorians, humility and humor were essential. The young man apparently departed instantly!

In another incident, a priest who was a member of the Oratory asked Fr. Neri for his blessing to begin wearing a hair shirt, a way of practicing the mortification of the flesh among priests and monks. Neri suspected the priest wished to admire his own holiness more than would be appropriate, so he responded yes, provided the penitent would wear the shirt on the outside of his regular clothes for a month first. There would be no self-deception in Neri's community. Can't help but think of St. Therese, right?

Neri saw humor as common sense, entirely fitting for those dealing with the human condition on earth, whether as priests or laymen. To take oneself too seriously was the greatest of sins. Philip is quoted as asserting "A cheerful and glad spirit attains to perfection much more readily than a melancholy spirit." But God must have greeted Philip Neri at the Gates of Heaven with a hearty chuckle, for he truly was the saint who "laughed his way to heaven." (It is unclear whether Philip brought the pet monkey, who often accompanied him while he preached, with him to the Pearly Gates).

These dynamics of self-deprecation, gentle humor, and humbleness are central to relationship building. When people never admit to weakness or errors, we find it difficult to trust them. No one is ever right all the time and we all understand this, at least at an unconscious level. When people we know to be knowledgeable and good thinkers admit that they don't know something, we give *more* credence to what they do say because we know they are willing to say so when they don't know something. Trust is essential in relationship building and it can only come through a good measure of humility on the part of both parties. In this spirit, you can become more tolerant of yourself, more accepting of your particular blind spots and, as we shall see, ultimately more able to live flexibly and generously with others. An occasional loss of agency, at the hands of Dame Folly, is an important capacity-building experience.

Philip Neri clearly appreciated the power and effectiveness of physical humor, which comes in as many variations as verbal humor. Each of us deals with a body on a daily basis, as noted earlier. We rely on this machine to make our way in the world, but it is often an unreliable vehicle for our mind and spirit. We each have a complex, multi-faceted relationship with this physical self. When it comes to building a shared self with another human being, bodies are shared intimately and so too are our feelings about our physical self. Physical humor can lubricate (sorry) these complex interactions, both with oneself and with a partner. There is no better illustration of physical humor (especially for couples) than the film *All of Me* starring two masters of the genre, Lily Tomlin and Steve Martin, in which they are accidently forced to share a single body!

Here are a couple of kinds of physical humor and an idea or two about the value they can provide. Slapstick humor usually involves a 'victim' whose body fails to navigate the physical world. When someone slips on a banana peel, he or she is temporarily rendered mechanical, prey to the forces of physics, and 'out of control.' Slapstick relies on this clash of mechanical and living action.[21]

---

[21] This idea is borrowed from the French philosopher Henri Bergson (1859–1941). It is elaborated, among many others, in a series of essays published in English as *Laughter*, published originally in 1900 in French as *Le Rire*.

This is, in a sense, a visual joke, where the loss of control we experience in a language joke is externalized. We laugh when the victim is momentarily rendered hapless. Timing is everything in slapstick, of course. If there is time for a viewer to feel concern that injury may have occurred, the humor is lost. But we know that Wile E. Coyote will survive his plunge over the cliff while chasing the Roadrunner to live another day so there is an absence of anxiety from the start. There is an instant catharsis. The incongruity of event and outcome produces pure amusement.

This kind of absurd incongruity can serve to remind us about the unreliability of our bodies, as much as we would like to believe otherwise. Young bodies are unreliable enough, but yours is guaranteed to become more so over the course of a loving partnership and so is your partner's. None of this matters, of course, as long as you have the kind of agency and sense of humor demonstrated by the shopkeeper during the Blitz. When one of your personal windows gets bombed unexpectedly, remember to see it for what it is… physical damage that doesn't define your self. A Warren Buffet old people's joke: Wife: "Let's go upstairs and make love!" Husband: "Make up your mind, dear. Which do you want to do?"

On an equally cheerful note, there is no more emotional time for a couple than when one member is carrying a child. Any couple fortunate enough to enjoy a healthy pregnancy together will do well to remember how humor can teach us to deal with our bodies. The physical changes, especially as the birth date approaches, will inevitably produce ample opportunities for slapstick moments, mostly unintended. Some gentle practiced humor concerning the vagaries of our physical selves, our gifts and our inevitable deficiencies, can be a source of kindness, emotional support and some healthy self-deprecation for the mother whose body is taken over by a mysterious internal entity with a mind of its own.

For all its benefits, however, humor has not always been acknowledged as an asset to virtuous behavior. Aristotle and Plato thought humor a rather base use of human mental capacity. Most religious figures make little use of it. Comedy has historically ranked lower on the scale of aesthetic achievement than drama, and so it goes. But humor has always been around to help us see ourselves in action. Remember *Lysistrata*, the fourth-century BC play by Aristophanes in which the women refuse all sex until the men stop fighting one war after the other? Talk about a mirror in which to see oneself.

Such unconventional thinking and acting works well to draw attention to convention itself. In so doing, it raises our awareness of when we are going through the motions and when we are engaging with the importance of the ritual. Humor offers a valuable support to a positive mindset. It is an important part of your armamentarium in the fight for self-awareness. It provides a mechanism that encourages optimism and agency, that essential power to control the story of who we are and how we operate in the world. It can be just what the doctor ordered to provide much needed insight into your own habits of mind by disrupting your automated thinking patterns. Seeing yourself in action can unlock your unconscious biases or blind spots.

These two benefits of humor create the basic building blocks for a balanced self with access to reason, strength and spirit. In the next two chapters, we look at additional habits for living that can free your spiritual dimension: your power of sustained attention and your imagination. We will see how humor pairs with attention to interrupt the flow of daily events and in so doing reminds us to shift focus beyond our transactional world. We will see how the 'playful' spirit of humor can pair with imagination to reset, to invent new directions as needed, on the expedition toward real love.

CHAPTER EIGHT

Attention

"Attention is the rarest and purest
form of generosity." Simone Weil

"The world is too much with us; late and soon.
Getting and spending, we lay waste our powers.
Little we see in Nature that is ours;
We have given our hearts away, a sordid boon!"
William Wordsworth (1807)

Humor provides a useful introduction to your tool kit for managing the challenges of a shared life. Because humor disrupts our 'automated' thinking processes, it increases self-awareness, particularly awareness of our unconscious 'habits of mind.' Self-awareness, in turn, combats self-deception. Use of your attention provides an additional tool for building a loving relationship. The term conveys the essential idea of "(at)tending" to the other (person), being alert to and caring for the needs and wants of your partner. The words we use to talk about our attention reveal that it is a precious commodity. You 'pay' attention to someone or something. You 'spend' time 'paying' attention. Attention— marshalling it, focusing it, distributing it, prioritizing it—requires you to use your agency. In a partnership, you must build a shared agency and with it a mutual commitment to prioritizing your attention to one another.

Attention also means concentrating, in a focused fashion, on a given topic or object. This is not easily accomplished under any circumstances, given our evolutionary background and the constant onslaught of information we face daily. It is particularly difficult when committed to 'attending to' one's partner as a first priority. What follows are a few thoughts about managing this challenge in a partnership.

Stephen Covey pointed out in his classic *The Seven Habits of Highly Effective People* (1989) that all of us need to focus more regularly on what is important, rather than what is urgent. This nugget of wisdom remains highly relevant and highly challenging. Attention, after all, is an evolutionary strategy dominated by physical needs. We are not built to automatically invest processing capacity in efforts to 'consider the lilies of the field,' or other similar abstractions. It is 'natural' to prioritize physical well-being. Think "OMG, that's a saber-toothed tiger over there! I need to split!" While there may be fewer saber-toothed tigers on the prowl today, there is more stuff than ever competing for your attention and promising endless rewards. Entertainment and distraction have been the name of the game over thousands of years. The Romans favored the lions versus the martyrs to fill the Colosseum. The medieval Church relied on staging colorful 'passion plays' on the steps of the town church before Mass. Pro sports, films, and TV command our collective 'viewings' and transform them into 'ratings.' Add in the ubiquitous 'screens' of today and our eyeballs have been commodified as never before. Everyone is buying and selling your attention at a furious rate day in and day out.[22]

In such an environment, attentional capacity can become perversely desensitized. The older we get, the more all the incoming seems like 'same old, same old.' Not only does this tendency provoke advertisers and entertainers to go to ever more outrageous lengths to capture attention, it also causes us to put more, not less, of our attention on autopilot. Such unconscious processing may improve our efficiency in dealing with ever more data, but this is the opposite response to what is needed if we are committed to 'spending' our attention on actively building a loving bond with a lifetime partner.

Screwtape is disdainful of humans' ability to control their attention. He points out gleefully to Wormwood that any time his patient has a moment of serious thought, particularly of the spiritual type so dangerous to devils, it is a simple matter to fire off a few hunger pangs or an urgent need for a bathroom break, and the thought will disappear instantly.

To fight back, committed partners must take control of their (shared) attention through the combination of self-awareness and will power. Attention must be paid to the objects and ideas that

---

[22] There exists a voluminous literature on 'mindfulness' with important insights and practical advice on controlling attention. We do not pretend to have mastered even a fraction of the material available. We did enjoy reviewing a bit of 'backlash' literature against the forces working to engage your attention with ever more grotesque diversions, generally to feed an algorithm that, in turn, generates more profit for the provider. See, for instance, Jenny Odell, *How To Do Nothing: Resisting the Attention Economy* (2019). Odell, an art teacher at Stanford, makes a robust call to exert control over your attention, in part by redefining notions of 'productivity.' See also her opinion piece "Finding Time in the Age of TikTok," *New York Times*, September 1, 2019.

will enhance the creation of a shared self with your partner. Trivia must not be allowed to dominate. This is our concern in this chapter. What are the ideas and objects that 'deserve' attention particularly from a couple? How might you and your partner use your shared attention to deepen your own coupledom?

Simply embracing the basic principle of paying attention to one another is a good starting point. The well-known researchers/ therapists John and Joan Gottman argue that couples who focus on each other are much less likely to divorce than those who don't. They note that when one partner makes a 'bid' for communication, something as casual as mentioning at the breakfast table that "I need to drop off my shirts at the laundry on my way to work today," his or her partner has three options. He/she can 'turn away' in their parlance, i.e. ignore the remark. He/she can 'turn against,' i.e. object or find fault with the remark. Or, he/she can 'turn toward' their partner by some form of positive acknowledgement of the remark. The researchers' data demonstrate that 'turning toward' behavior is much more frequent in successful coupledom. [23]

Fair enough. There is certainly nothing more painful than observing a married couple in a restaurant who seem to have nothing to say to one another. But there is much more to attention than simply acknowledging the other's conversational gestures. Attention can offer a 'window' into the thoughts and feelings of your chosen partner. Where and how a person deploys attention reveals much about their priorities and thinking processes. This is vital information for a partner building a shared relationship. For instance, we have found that the idea of paying attention to something 'beautiful' is a revealing opportunity. Bear with us for a moment. This is not as abstract or silly as it might seem in a busy

---

[23] The Gottmans' work is summarized in a general way by Catherine Pearson in "How Long Does It Take to Fix a Marriage?" in the *New York Times*, September 27, 2022.

world. When a couple is building their coupledom through the habit of attention, we propose focusing together on an idea or an object. While the possibilities are endless, we recommend 'beauty' as a focus of attention because of its simultaneous elusiveness and practicality.

Despite overuse of the term, everyone has an idea of what they think is beautiful. Each partner in a couple hopefully feels that their beloved is 'beautiful,' ideally both physically and spiritually. When a person sees or hears something that strikes them as 'beautiful,' they have a mysterious but unmistakable response. A couple will find that identifying this response and exploring it together can produce insights about the thought processes and values of the 'other' (and maybe for yourself as well!). Moreover, because most couples share a physical space over time, they have a natural opportunity to decide together on how to make their shared space 'beautiful' or at least as attractive as possible. Everyone knows the jokes about trying to wallpaper a bathroom with your partner and how the experience will test your love, patience and commitment. But seriously, the challenge starts with *choosing* the wallpaper to begin with. It is one of the ultimate learning experiences for a couple to engage on what each of you considers attractive, or more grandly, beautiful. Such knowledge opens the door to more challenging topics such as answering the question "why" do you think this or that is beautiful? Why is blue your favorite color? This may seem a strange way to focus your attention, especially if you as a couple are not accustomed to such probing conversations, but we can assure you that there is much to gain through this use of your shared attention.

You are actually probing to activate consideration of those moments that link you individually and collectively to the spiritual dimension of life. Beauty may be an abstract idea, but it won't take long to realize that both you and your partner recognize beauty as very real. You will inevitably end up talking about how you feel when engaged with something beautiful, a song perhaps, or a painting, or an antique kitchen table.

Those reactions are important to recognize and examine as a source of (ideally) shared happiness. The more you become aware of the sources and impact of these reactions, the better you will become at bringing happiness to your partner. Beauty is the 'bridge' from your transactional universe to a glimpse of transcendence. How can we justify such a bold claim? Well, beauty is a unique category of human experience. It exists, for lack of a better description, with one foot in the infinite, transcendent domain and the other in the physical finite world. Beauty is not subject to the ravages of time. The beauty of an object or a person is, in the mind of the beholder, incorruptible. Beautiful things, whether paintings, symphonies, poems, icons, and mosaics or flowers, mountain peaks, birds, trees and waterfalls, contain the potential to inspire, at least momentarily, a sense of perfection. So too do exemplary acts of kindness, generosity, bravery and self-sacrifice on the part of our fellow humans. It is as though morality, i.e. doing the 'right thing,' has an aesthetic dimension. Doing or witnessing generous and kind actions somehow provokes the same kind of happiness, or positivity, that we experience when we encounter and engage with the 'beautiful.' Engaging forms of beauty—beautiful objects, beautiful actions—invites a 'glimpse' beyond the material world to those willing to 'pay' attention. The rational, transactional mind struggles to find a category that captures 'the beautiful' but we are each endowed with the capacity to recognize examples of such a special quality.

When you think about it, our suggestion is really not particularly radical. Every culture and race has used beauty to inspire, to explore, and to provoke since the beginning of time. It offers an ideal escape from the noisy efforts to dominate your attention.

The logical first step in exercising control over your (shared) attention is to reduce the flow of inputs that require processing. This is hardly a novel idea but it makes very good sense and is in keeping with our belief in the importance of 'resets' and pivots discussed in Part One. We propose finding time together to step back, withdraw, retreat, seek shelter from the endless stimuli, and do so on a regular basis. It is not easy to find time, especially together, especially with two jobs and kids, but the habit will pay important dividends. Schedule the time together and stick to it. Anywhere will do, of course, but the experience will be enhanced if a location can be found that promotes your shared goal of connecting to the transcendent dimension of reality. Ideally, in addition to eliminating intrusive, attention-seeking stimuli, the space should be 'beautiful' in the sense that it inspires or hints at non-transactional values. Here are a couple of examples to illustrate what we mean.

There is a reason that the interiors of churches and temples and mosques are called the 'sanctuary.' Such spaces are designed to encourage 'communion,' the unification of the visitor with a larger reality beyond the material world. Great churches, such as the cathedrals of Europe, were built intentionally as inspirational spaces. They seek to provoke a sense of wonder and humility in the visitor by their sheer size/volume and intricate decoration. Monumental mosques offer similar spaces that also rely on size and exquisite decoration to induce such sentiments. While size does matter, many sanctuary spaces offer a carefully constructed multi-sensory experience as well, through their decorative elements (sculptures, paintings, mosaics, frescoes, stained glass and the like), their musical offerings, and, in some cases, their distinctive smells of candles and incense.[24]

---

[24] Eastern and western religions have long recognized the importance of attention, both by offering spaces that are conducive to focus, and offering guidance on how attention should be structured and managed,

Another traditional option to support transcendent thinking is space in the natural world. Mankind has always been challenged to outdo Mother Nature when it comes to creating space for inspired attention. Think of the hermits of the Greco-Roman era, the Islamic marabouts of Mohammad's time, or the 'transcendentalist' painters in the American southwest in the twentieth century. The 'patient' in *The Screwtape Letters* retreats to an abandoned country mill with a 'good book' in hand to ponder his love life (and ultimately chooses the more spiritual of his potential partners over the more cynical). And, lest you think that such so-called 'romantic' traditions have finally died off, we offer two examples encountered in our research that demonstrate the continuing power of Nature to provoke a sense of transcendence. A recent *New Yorker* magazine article[25] profiles the influential and prolific philosopher Daniel Dennett (who worries about the origins of consciousness among other things) who has 'retreated' to an island off the coast of Maine. This remarkable polymath is portrayed gazing wistfully at blue sky from the end of his dock at the conclusion of the essay. The author does not speculate whether Dennett is, in fact, drifting from the 'materialist' beliefs for which he is well known, but it looks a lot like he is feeding his spirit through Mother Nature!

Another unlikely contemporary example of the search for spiritual awakening through nature is found in *Why We Can't Sleep* (2019), an empathetic (and snarky) look at the tribulations of female Gen Xers. The author, Ada Calhoun, concludes her compendium of

---

often through meditation. It goes without saying that a couple working to develop their shared attentional skills could profit from these sources and traditions, which have been used to bring worshippers' attention to 'the face of God' (as the Psalmist says) for thousands of years. Any couple with the good fortune to share a religious faith or to have committed to building a shared faith can take advantage of these traditions and exercises.

[25] "A Science of the Soul" by Joshua Rothman, March 27, 2017.

depressing vignettes by describing herself in a Walmart parking lot. With an apparent lack of irony, she gazes toward the blue sky overhead in search of a ray of hope or inspiration or perhaps solace amid her testing daily life.

Both Calhoun and Dennett are surely more agnostic than believing, more analytical than spiritual, yet they default, spontaneously and unapologetically, to 'mother nature' for some sign of larger meaning or purpose. They summon the power of that Irving Berlin standard..."blue skies, smilin' at me...nothing but blue skies do I see...." Maybe they see that smile when they look up. Maybe you and your loved one will too. We hope so.[26]

In addition to manmade objects and the natural world, our aesthetic sense can also be activated by exposure to so-called 'uplifting' behaviors. This source of 'beauty' should not be overlooked. Consider that special feeling when you encounter, with your full attention, a beautiful object or natural setting and how similar it is to your reaction when you witness an act of kindness or generosity. It is inspiring, uplifting. It provokes optimism and tranquility. Whether you witness such positive actions in person or through the media, it is important to pay attention to them, to record your reaction and to share it with your loved one.

Consider paying careful attention to such 'positive' dimensions of your growing love as well as to potential problem areas. It is, of course, vital to confront challenging areas. For instance, committing to the discipline of assessing your decision-making as a couple can often lead to productive insights into hidden

---

[26] For a summary of current scientific research on the power of the natural environment to promote mental and physical health, see https://depts. washington.edu/hhwb/, a report titled *Green Cities: Good Health*. Pope Francis asserts that care of the natural environment is a spiritual obligation for the Catholic faithful. See *Laudato Si: Care of our Common Home* (2015).

problems that can retard your growth as a couple. You may want to ask "Do I/we always think in terms of winning and losing in all situations?" "Do we judge our behavior (or that of others) on purely self-centered terms?" "Do we pretend otherwise?" But it is equally important and productive to recall and discuss the best moments, those occasions when a special sense of pleasure and satisfaction is provoked by a shared encounter of beauty (try moving beyond discussions of the quality of orgasms!).

By accessing these domains (and bringing our full attention to them), a couple cultivates engagement with a sense of awe and humility. Such moments support the existence of the transcendent or spiritual dimension of life in which genuine coupledom exists. We invented a tiny ritual as a new couple that became, without a lot of understanding at the time, a central construct in our shared use of attention. It is a building block of vital importance in our shared being. Claire describes the origin of our so-called 'golden moments':

> I remember holding hands walking home from Dante class to Highland Avenue the week we started reviewing for finals. We were discussing Canto V of the *Inferno*, featuring literature's most famous lovers (at least for Italians!), Francesca and Paolo. We laughed when you said how we could be modern versions of Dante's young couple in love: "Right now, walking to class together in a bit of a winter breeze, it's kind of like the wind that pursued them eternally. And like them, we are so in love." (If you are wondering why this young couple happen to be ensconced in Hell, we recommend checking out Dante's *Divine Comedy*.)
>
> Now I realize that this may have been our first Golden Moment, a concept that we would not

identify as such until our honeymoon two years later. Gradually we recognized golden moments as our 'glimpses' of transcendence, extraordinary joys in ordinary moments, to be noted and stored. The trick is to *notice and pay attention* to the glimpse of transcendence when it occurs in ordinary time.

One of us simply says 'golden moment' and a 'spiritual selfie' is captured. I began to call them "Golden Moments" in the diary I was keeping during our honeymoon. So early on we captured one fleeting moment at a time, not big deal lovemaking or celebrating our one month anniversary, but being served a glass of white wine with breakfast at a modest country inn outside Paris, walking into Santa Maria Novella in Florence hand in hand, or sipping coffee in bed under a huge feather blanket in Fluelen, Switzerland, on a freezing cold morning in August!

Over a lifetime, these become a shared shorthand of delight beyond the present time and space. We have these spiritual selfies of ourselves playing Monopoly or making clay Christmas tree ornaments with our kids, or playing astronaut and fighting off the invading Visigoths with our four year old grandson. These moments aren't a way to remember the first time you see your baby's face, or your wedding day first dance. Those moments you will never forget. Golden moments are ordinary bits of life that evoke a shared awareness of our oneness as a couple.

After 56 years we have quite a spectacular number of golden moments. I had never thought of them all together even once over all these years. I had never considered how they have sprinkled transcendent joy and spiritual reality throughout our lives. Until now.

The opportunity to share moments of joy with another person is precious. Thoughtful couples often embrace a favorite song or location for its significance to their coupledom. Through the exchange of rings or other symbolic gifts, they create special objects invested (one hopes) with transcendent (intangible) value. The material value of such tokens seems extraneous to us, as only the jeweler can profit from such spending. The value of the object can increase over time only if the love does. So it is important to keep investing in your shared spirit, to identify and 'immortalize' those intangible shared experiences.

In fairness, managing shared attention in coupledom is not easy. The uses of attention in the pursuit of coupledom are relatively easy to describe, but challenging to execute faithfully and consistently. We have used the term 'habits of mind' on purpose to underscore the need for repetition, for practice of attention so that it becomes deeply embedded in the shared consciousness of the couple. Book stores are well-stocked with advice on structuring one's attentional behavior, whether through yoga, meditation, communion, or twelve step programs. All recommend some kind of ritual or repetitive behavior, either alone or in groups. In all cases, the goal is to override the fragmentation of attention through a proscribed exercise of structured thinking. We are agnostic on these options, but totally committed to their objective, the ongoing and active management of one's attention in partnership with a loved one.

Of course this focus on attention comes with the ever present risk of self-deception, as C.S. Lewis is quick to point out. The devils are never far away and always capable of trickery that makes even the best of intentions go off the rails. Even careful and extended engagement with our favorite topic of attention, beauty, can fail miserably. Recall the sad letter from 'Name Withheld'? Her initially inspiring and gratifying engagement with 'beauty' as a photo editor has degraded over the years. She's lost 'that lovin' feeling,' to quote the Righteous Brothers back in 1965. The unique power of beauty to inspire and energize has been replaced by a deadening void of doubt and regret. Certainly we can agree that she has encountered a common problem in controlling one's attention while avoiding self-deception. She has fallen prey to 'conventional thinking' about beauty. As with virtually every domain of thought today, there are media-based, self-appointed tastemakers who specialize in bestowing their blessings on fashions and trends and schools of thought.

'Groupthink' is alive and well as a source of self-deception. Anyone wishing to be part of a group will feel pressure, consciously or not, to align with group values. Attention will be consumed by those objects or ideas preferred by the group whether a given painting style, fashion trend, musical genre, or virtually anything else for that matter. It is not easy to buck the trend. But the search by a couple for the experiences that offer glimpses of a larger, non-material world cannot be outsourced. Your conscience and (shared) consciousness can and should make you wary of unconsciously embracing group values. Name Withheld seems to have forgotten that beauty, in particular, exists in the material world *and* the spiritual world. Discussions and experiences of this topic will inevitably seem paradoxical or doubt provoking on occasion. It is then that you will know that you are getting closer to the real thing![27]

One final observation about the use of your attention. We have two grown children and five grandkids varying in age from eight to sixteen. For a couple committed to a lifelong partnership, children are a natural and very important part of the equation. They may be the gift that keeps on costing, but most couples consider their kids *the* most important element of their shared life. They dominate the focus and attention of their parents to a remarkable degree (sometimes to the detriment of the couple!). In many cases, parents find themselves for the first time acting in genuinely selfless ways with *all* their attention invested in providing security, well-being and love for the kids. The feelings generated by the birth of a couple's child may well be their greatest opportunity to glimpse something approaching a miracle in the midst of our material, transactional daily life.

This devotion is as it should be, of course, for small children are essentially totally dependent on their parents. Such commitment often carries forward over decades with tiger moms and helicopter parents taking charge of the well-being of their offspring to a sometimes frightening (and destructive) degree. There is little doubt in our (shared) mind that parenting is among the most valuable and educational experiences that a couple can hope to

---

[27] At this point, David really wanted to do a (slightly) wonky overview of the history of ideas of beauty in the West—the classical versus the romantic versus the 'modern'—as these notions show up in everything from music to architecture, in order to offer some material to kick around if and when you actually try using your attentional power to talk about beauty with your loved one. But that idea got voted down in part because he knows nothing about Eastern concepts of beauty and it came off as unbalanced. There is a brief (unbalanced) appendix if you are dying to know more about characters like Nietzsche, Kant, Stendhal, and even a group of radical American Black quiltmakers!

share. Each child certainly deserves the complete and undivided attention of (ideally) two parents, and their every possible effort to understand the child as he or she matures physically and mentally and spiritually. In bringing their full attention to the child, the parents always risk the possibility of conflict and misunderstanding, both with the child and with each other. Parenting is a shared experience and a shared responsibility. Attention to a child offers a particularly large window into the self of each parent and as such, it offers a powerful opportunity to the partners' understanding of one another and their shared coupledom. Every shared parenting decision can deepen the shared self the couple is building. Ideally, parenting does not end at some magical moment. Learning from and with grown children, and occasionally glimpsing traces of your parenting efforts when this adult was a child (for better or worse) is another learning experience for a couple.

In summary, your ability to focus your attention is a critical asset in the creation of coupledom. Focus requires self-awareness to appreciate how your attention is accustomed to operating on autopilot, and how you must consciously take control. A suitable environment can assist in this process, as can the use of a variety of rituals or practices. Encounters with beauty can offer glimpses of the transcendent possibilities each of us should strive to embrace. Beauty in all its variations, natural, manmade, physical and behavioral, is a vast domain filled with conventions, radical thinkers and Luddites of the first order. It is never simple to fish in such big oceans of thought. But if you and your partner are willing to seek inspiration and stimulation for a sense of the transcendent together, we offer attention to beauty as a logical place to start your search. One of the joys of coupledom is having a (trusted) partner with whom to share the challenge of overcoming your natural self-deceptive tendencies.

There remains one additional tactic needed to mobilize

the spiritual potential of coupledom and that is the power of imagination. The final step after self-awareness (through humor) and spiritual energy (through attention) is liberation through imagination. What do you *do* with spiritual glimpses? How can such moments be transformed into actions in your life? Your high functioning imagination will become the final piece of the puzzle. Your agency will be complete and activated. You (and your partner) will be empowered to define your future together, no matter what events may occur.

CHAPTER NINE

Imagination

"Grown-ups ask for too many
explanations. They have done too much
history, math and grammar. It is not
their fault if they learn slowly."
Antoine de Saint-Exupéry[28]

"The test of a first-rate intelligence is the ability
to hold two opposed ideas in mind at the same
time and still retain the ability to function..."
F. Scott Fitzgerald

Imagination provides the power to break the bounds of material
reality, to think outside the box, to enlarge your world (and that
of your partner) so that transcendent love can flourish. You can
create the 'meaning' and value of your shared experiences, rather
than allowing others to do so for you or succumbing to passive
victimhood when the fates conspire against you. You can expand
the 'glimpses' of a larger reality that your efforts with sustained

---

[28] *The Little Prince* (1943). The Prince is explaining why an adult to whom
he shows his drawing of an elephant swallowed by a python misidentifies
the picture as "an old hat."

attention have hopefully produced. Imagination is the secret weapon to control your shared life, to strengthen the optimism and idealism that are essential to your joyful partnership. Here is Claire's example of imaginative 'agency' in action:

> One afternoon, one of my younger female colleagues asked me what it was like to be a grandmother. Never at a loss for words (just candor), I told her it was exhilarating. (The Pinocchio in me recoiled at the direction the conversation was taking.) The inevitable question "How so?" did, however, trigger a memory that gave me the perfect answer.
>
> "Well," I breathed, "for a change, I won't be the first woman to do my new job as a grannie! I already have a great role model."
>
> The next thing I knew I was regaling my friend with stories of my own grandmother (Bis-nonna's daughter, remember?). She had been a magical force throughout my early life. I remember when we were all at dinner at her damask linen-covered dining room table. I was probably seven or eight. The little kids each had a tiny cordial glass with a teaspoon of red wine in it. I knocked mine over reaching for it. Terror seized me as the stigmata wounded the white linen. My father's voice thundered my name. I froze. Nonna announced: "How beautiful! We have just received a blessing from God on our table and on the whole family! Thank you, dear Lord, for this blessing! We rejoice with You!" A bit of salt and a small damp towel dealt with the blessing while people began to recall funny stories of past family

dinner spills. My well-deserved correction never happened. By the way, how had I managed to bring a blessing from God?

See what we mean by agency? Mind over matter and only meaning matters. S/he who controls the meaning defines the matter: the past, the present and the future. Joy is ours to create and our imaginations have the power to make it happen.

Let's take a closer look at this wonderful gift of imagination. It is another 'habit of mind,' like humor and attention, that enables us to control (at least a little bit) how our brain operates. Imagination can be deployed to deal with our brains' tendency to sort ideas and experiences into categories and keep them there. Imagine (sorry!) a cataloguing system that sorts books into 'topics' such as fiction or non-fiction, biography or current events. There are always problems with such systems because lots of books don't fit into a single category, or the librarian chooses category A when the writer intended category B, and on and on. But sorting ideas and information into categories is essential for our brains to operate, just as are the automating functions we encountered when discussing humor and attention. The trick is to recognize how the system operates and 'work' to maintain flexibility and porosity among the categories. That way, no idea gets lost forever simply because it got 'shelved' in some obscure category. And, every now and then, things classified as 'bad' (wine spills on white tablecloths) can be re-catalogued as 'good' (a blessing from God).

Flexible, creative thinking is clearly an asset in many situations, but it is a challenge to maintain. As we gather more experience, our categories become more fixed and the power of our imagination is challenged. The danger of self-deception is never far away, because we become unaware of the categories our brains are using and/or how rigid these 'buckets' have become. To illustrate this phenomenon, consider for a moment the crossword puzzle. Good puzzles require more than a big vocabulary and random factual knowledge to solve. Puzzle authors exploit rigid brain categories by presenting clues that point resolutely to one kind of answer. For instance, what possible answers come to mind when you read the following clue: "a six letter word for 'Post box contents?'" A good puzzle solver must cultivate a fluid mindset, an ability to shift frames of reference constantly to avoid being 'blinded' by category power. The answer, BTW, is at the end of the chapter.

We mentioned our children and grandchildren in the previous chapter. Imagination is one of many gifts provided by children to their parents (and grandparents and other adults as well). Children are very good at being 'imaginative.' They have very 'weak' or fungible categories because they don't have much experience/data to work with. What is 'real' or 'make believe'? Where does 'long ago' end and 'today' begin? Is there a line where animals end and 'humans' begin? What is 'close by' as opposed to 'far away'? Children's categories are easily broken down and resorted into new and 'imaginative' groupings. Children enjoy the gift of 'fluid imagination,' moving with great ease from 'reality' to 'fantasy' and back. They can slip the bonds of daily routines to generate a wide world of make believe. Naturally, we have to tell you a story about our grandchildren and their imaginations. Did you really think you'd get through this whole thing without another grandchild story? Here we go… with their 'nonna' doing some coaching.

> One day, after I had read a story to my first grandson, I asked him whether he would like to act out the story together. "Really, Nonna? Could we do that?" "Sure," I said, "we have read it so many times. I bet you know the parts already. Do you want to be the Mouse or the Lion?"

Soon my three-year-old Mouse is on the rug looking for seeds to bring home to his new baby mice. On the sofa, he sees a promising huge bushy thing (me!). He crawls up to look for the seeds that must be hidden on it. Crash! The bushy thing rises up and roars! "How dare you walk on me? I am the king of beasts! You are a tiny, useless *mouse*! I will eat you for a snack!!!"

And so Aesop's (and LaFontaine's) great fable of the Lion and the Mouse begins and we own it already. After a few 'role plays' together, Alex is filled with ideas about improving the story. After pretending to gnaw through the ropes with his sharp teeth and free the lion from the cruel trap, set (in this contemporary version of the story) by some guys in a truck, Alex proposes: "the grateful lion could actually invite the Mouse and his babies to meet the Lion's cubs, right, Nonna? The little guys could become friends since their dads are now buddies, right?" "Sure," I said.

"But wait, Nonna, how about the guys and their truck, and their traps and their ropes??? They would be on the road soon again to trap other lions and kill them or sell them, right???"

Alex the Mousie has a plan. He could sneak under the truck engine, and bite a few holes in the tiny hoses that connect the gas tank to the engine! "Yes! No gas for the engine!" "Then the lion could push that truck over the edge of the ravine so it would crash all the way down to the huge rocks and its wheels would break off." "Nonna, then the men would have to walk miles and miles to get back to their camp. And their truck would be wrecked forever." "Right, no more Daddy Lions will be in danger from those guys... ever..."

Talk about agency! Aesop's imaginary universe keeps right on growing. Eventually the kid and I make tickets that he sells to his parents and friends and the next show goes big time in the living room... the crowd goes wild. In one showing, the little kid is the lion and is, of course, scary and tough and super confident. When he falls into the rope trap, he becomes afraid and then very, very excited and grateful when freed by the super sharp teeth of the Dad-mouse. (That would be me!) In the second 'on demand' showing, the little kid acts out the brave mousey who responds instantly to the roar of the lion when he falls into the trap. So, this time, it's the little kid who quickly explains to the huge lion the reason why he should not eat the mousey... "You see, sometimes even very small friends can bring very big help." Not a bad insight from a very little kid.

The child's powers of imagination expand a great story. He enjoys a wonderful feeling of competence and control that is rare for little kids (and for many adults as well). Even better, he inspires the adults around him to shake off their own narrow roles, their concrete shoes that anchor them to 'reality.' Wouldn't such a person make a wonderful partner someday?

Adults who are able to maintain such fluidity between categories of 'real' and 'imagined,' of invention and reinvention, of self and circumstance, are often well-equipped to create new things, new ideas. We tend to think of such people as 'creative types,' artists and poets and the like. Many artists talk about their efforts to stay in touch with their 'inner child' (see the quote at the beginning of this chapter). Some talented thinkers are able to cross-pollinate such seemingly disparate fields as science, medicine, spirituality and fantasy. Consider the professional mathematician (and Anglican priest) Charles Dodgson (Lewis Carroll), who authored *Alice in Wonderland*. Our beloved C.S. Lewis wrote the fanciful *Chronicles of Narnia*, while masquerading as an Oxbridge scholar of European Literature. Or scientists such as Albert Schweitzer, the humanitarian physician and authority on the organ music of J.S. Bach, and geneticist Francis Collins, the former head of the National Institutes of Health who recently penned *The Language of God*, a reflection on spirituality through scientific research. You probably know someone who makes connections between ideas or people or things (or all of the above) that leave you scratching your head. Imagination is like that.

Here is a quick illustration from David's experience teaching a course on 'The Creative Process' many years ago:

> I once co-taught an undergraduate seminar entitled 'The Creative Process' at Indiana University with a colleague from the German Department. The seminar was hardly 'creative' because the two faculty members were not. We put together some readings *about* the creative process, having no ability to demonstrate the concept ourselves. We read *The Act of Creation* by Arthur Koestler and his opening story has stuck with me all these years. He describes Archimedes, the Greek mathematician who lived in Sicily around 250 BC, and who is credited with solving a bunch of brain-teasing problems. How could one 'measure' the volume of

an irregular object, in this case a crown of gold that the King feared had been adulterated with other metals? Settling into his bathtub one evening, Archimedes had his 'eureka!' moment. The water rose in the tub as he jumped in, as it always did, but for the first time, he realized that the water was rising (being displaced) by exactly the volume of his body (assuming he got entirely under the water!) The problem is actually more complicated, related to principles of flotation and the density of various metals, but it doesn't matter. Nor does it matter that Archimedes supposedly ran naked through the streets proclaiming 'eureka' (I found it!) following the bathtub moment.

Koestler's point is that Archimedes had connected a math problem to his bathtub, an example of creativity connecting two disparate domains. Doing so required a couple of important psychological capacities: focus/attention and cross-pollination of mental categories.

Focus, in this particular case, involves the mathematician's extended efforts to solve this seemingly intractable problem. Consciously and eventually unconsciously he was engaged; he was pondering, and he reached a point where he was 'ripe' for an imaginative insight. The final step crossed over from one of the brain's sorting buckets, math problems, to another (behavior of water in a tub).

OK…. all well and good, but what does any of this have to do with love? with creating lasting coupledom? We see two fundamental elements of transcendent love at work in the exercise of imagination. Not only does it provide the power of agency, the 'juice' for optimism about the future by its ability to generate positive meaning from different kinds of events. It also produces the flexible thinking that allows a couple to keep moving ahead, learning and sharing, rather than getting stuck in predictable (and perhaps self-deceptive) practices. If marriage is a conversation, as noted in an earlier chapter, imagination powers that dialogue toward new insights, rather than one big closed loop.

We have some experience with keeping the conversation moving ahead through imagination, and it started, remarkably enough, on our honeymoon. Or maybe even before.

We had a built-in advantage given our shared interest in 'imaginative' material (that is, French and European Literature). We were studying some of the greatest works of human imagination: writers such as Dante, Flaubert and even Bossuet, a seventeenth-century French cardinal known as a gifted essayist and sermonizer. (In grad school, David actually wrote an entire sermon on marriage imitating Bossuet for a seminar studying style in the French language. Claire liked it! Maybe it even sold her on the proposition?)

Whatever the case, we started out with a shared professional interest in understanding great ideas and beautiful writing. We had endless conversations as we struggled to use our imaginations to produce insightful analyses of these texts. How did we apply these emerging skills to our shared life? Well, our first venture as a married couple demonstrated an uncanny faith in the power of imagination. Not for us a honeymoon at an 'all-inclusive resort' where every day guaranteed good food and endless celebration in some adult Disneyland. *We* took our $2000 and bought two tickets to Paris, reserved a rental car, and spent one night in a tourist hotel. That was it. The rest (eighty nine more days, to be precise) was an ongoing act of creation. Where to go? Where to sleep? Where to eat? What to *do*?

To be honest, we did intend to get to southern Italy (where Claire had relatives) sooner or later, and we hoped to get to England and Scotland (where David had relatives) at some point, but that was it for a plan. To be even more honest, it was not until we began to work on this opus, 54 years post honeymoon, that it occurred to us to wonder about our planning. We had somehow accumulated so much trust and confidence in our short courtship that it never occurred to us to question whether we could pull off such a 'vacation' together. From a distance it sounds like a disaster waiting to happen. But with one exception, we never encountered a wobble in our (shared) wheel.

Each day was an adventure created from scratch, as they say, and, given our limited resources, we could not rely on a secret booklet of travelers checks to bail us out if we screwed up. Find a cheap and peaceful hotel, find a good place for dinner and a source of provisions for lunchtime sandwiches and something to see somewhere off the beaten path. Claire's miraculous skills with the Michelin 'guide rouge' kept us well-fed and well-slept on our (less than) five dollars a day.

And that one genuine disaster? Of course it involved food, once again. This time, having successfully navigated two months of daily creativity from Paris to Marseille to Florence to Naples and back through Milan and Switzerland to Paris, we dumped the rental car and flew to London, arriving late in the evening with, of course, no plan or reservation. We trained into London and wandered the streets near the central railroad station searching for a bed and breakfast place for the night, but there was no room for us in any inn. Luggage in tow, we headed to the train station and booked onto the overnight train to Edinburgh, Scotland. Arriving in the wee hours of the morning, tired and very hungry, we sought food at the first place we encountered which happened to be the cafeteria of a well-known department store on the High Street. Still toting our luggage, we examined the unfamiliar offerings of peas on toast, beans on toast, and various puddings (i.e. sausages). Claire opted for an item called minced meat which, when she presented her tray, turned out to be very well-done hamburger meat floating in a watery gravy ladled over mashed potato. Having been clearly spoiled by our continental experience during which even the most unpromising roadside dives had consistently delivered tasty food (homemade pasta with local red sauce, for instance) for a pittance, Claire lost it on the spot. She broke into tears and fled to the nearest ladies room and refused to come out to face her plated choice. For several tenuous hours, it seemed as though we were reliving the near-fatal experience in Bloomington with the bags of iceberg lettuce and bottled dressing.

We did survive of course but Scotland on a budget, let's be candid, was not an ideal match for Claire's Mediterranean constitution. We found a B&B run by the stout Mrs. Campbell for a 'pound a night,' about $2.50. However, it required several of our precious shillings to be fed into a fireplace insert each night to keep the room temperature above 50 degrees in August. We did get a hearty and tasty cooked breakfast with the room each morning, although it also came with a testy stream of chatter from the proprietor about weak-kneed Americans when we complained about the cold. The stout woolen cardigan sweater in brown that David bought for Claire failed the style test and hasn't been seen in decades.

All this, we now see, was basic training for what real life had in store for us. Finding a hotel in a guidebook in some obscure town was one thing, but figuring out how to stay true to our so-called 'core values' as a couple making our way in the world was, it turned out, a true test of imagination. We had our shared 'pivot foot' firmly planted from the beginning. We would each have careers (not just jobs, but genuine, meaningful work that made a difference for others). We would have children and raise them better than we had been raised (sure, in your 20s you think you really know all the mistakes your parents made raising you!), *and*, most importantly, we would *not be separated from one another* in the pursuit of said careers.

These values were tested immediately as we approached the completion of our PhDs and headed to the job market in search of assistant professorships, ideally at an institution that at least a few people had heard of. There were, however, *way* too many newly minted PhDs in languages and literatures for the number of job opportunities available. Two classmates who, like us, had married, did get jobs, one in New Hampshire, one in Texas. Another married couple got one job; he accepted it, she left her professional goals and followed him. Another classmate abandoned ship in favor of an MBA program that promised to retrofit humanists for the real world. And we had our own complications. Claire was a year behind David in completing her degree, having dropped out for a year (to help her pregnant Mom). We had no additional fellowship or teaching assistantship support, *and* we had a kid! Things did not look good when David got no follow up interview at Sam Houston State!

So, imagination to the rescue. We loved IU and the students we had taught over the years as teaching assistants. Many were exceptionally bright and serious about learning. But IU was and is a *big* school, medicine, business, music, and law as well as arts and sciences. Tens of thousands of students. Big, big sports in the Big Ten. Big Greek scene and big parties. Undergrads, particularly freshmen, often had huge classes taught by brand new young teachers like us, teaching assistants. It was easy to get lost. We had never faced these challenges at Connecticut College or Princeton.

We occasionally talked about how great it would be if IU could somehow provide a small, liberal arts college-like experience so more of the academically motivated kids could find one another. We had heard that the University of Michigan had something called an Honors College within the University. Why not IU and why not *us* to create it??

Once the idea was hatched, Claire went into high gear as only she can to spin out our vision into a real possibility. We crafted a plan to take over a beautiful old limestone dormitory complete with its own dining hall. We called our idea the Living Learning Center. Incoming frosh would apply to live in the Center where there would be special seminars, clubs, guests and even student teaching opportunities. There would be a faculty advisory board, of course, and students could nominate the University's most popular faculty to teach courses in the Center, and, best of all, they would have *us* as faculty in residence!

Our commitment was to give the admitted students more opportunities to shape their academic lives, learn from their peers, and garner some personal attention. Claire even imagined inviting small groups of students to cook Sunday night supper with us when the dining hall was closed. Which eventually she did, producing many memorable kitchen moments in our apartment off the main lounge of the dorm, such as "Hey, Claire, this is amazing! I never knew you could *make* soup." (Inspired by the children's book *Stone Soup*, we had asked each attendee to bring one vegetable to dinner.)

So we went to work to sell our idea to the administration. Thanks to a happy set of circumstances, we completed the deal over the course of several months. The University Provost proved a big fan of the idea and even volunteered to chair the faculty advisory committee. The dorm we were asking for had become (unbeknown to us) the chosen home of the University's men's swimming and diving team. The glory they brought to themselves and the University in those days (around 1970) in the form of multiple NCAA championships and multiple Olympic gold medals (remember Mark Spitz, anyone?) had generated, shall we say, a rather celebratory culture in said dorm. The Director of Residential Life and other campus authorities were clearly shopping for a non-confrontational solution. Perhaps a Living Learning Center could help. So it happened! David became an assistant dean in the College of Arts and Sciences and director of the LLC and Claire became the head of residential life for the dorm, overseeing the work of the Resident Advisors who lived on each floor. (Yes, career stereotyping was alive and well in the late '60s and Claire was a hero to buy into her role.) We moved in with our three-year-old in tow, and set about the hard work of making all those idealistic claims a reality for the first group of admits. We got at least some of it right as the IU LLC will celebrate its 50th anniversary next year!

Thus began a shared lifetime of inventing ways to stick with our core values. The trust and admiration we built for one another through the shared creation of the LLC served us well. This opportunity proved to be the only time in our shared life that we both received job offers in the same place at the same time! On all subsequent career steps, one of us became the dreaded 'trailing spouse' (a dispiriting term if there ever was one). More about these challenges in the next chapter. For now, we want to underscore the importance of imagination, in both career decisions and personal decisions.

Out-of-the-box thinking was the only way to stay together and keep moving forward. When Claire followed David to the

University of Pennsylvania, she did so without a formal work offer. She reinvented herself as a foreign language pedagogy specialist and management consultant for higher education. Eight years later, she was named president of her alma mater. David followed Claire to Connecticut without a job and ended up joining the research division of Pfizer, Inc., the pharmaceutical company, from which he retired as head of scientific knowledge management.

Most importantly, we each integrated our own experience in self-reinvention into our careers as educators. We both worked without traditional job descriptions for decades, but somehow our 'work' always turned out to be a variation on the theme of imagination. We wanted others to see how powerful the exercise of personal imagination can be. We wanted to show our students that categorical thinking need not dominate their work or personal lives. Claire developed a curriculum for MBA students at the Wharton School that put language and cultural knowledge at the heart of their business training. She created multiple multidisciplinary centers at Conn that broke up the traditional discipline-based curricular structure and challenged students to connect hands-on personal experience to their academic interests. David built an international system of knowledge sharing across departments and therapeutic areas among the research scientists at Pfizer.

Insights are most frequently found at the intersections of very different realms of thought, and to generate such insights, it is essential to break traditional frames of reference. In our own ways we each embraced this fundamental truth about ideas. We had plenty of practice finding new ways to use our prior knowledge when we shifted from one professional domain to another, and we, perhaps unconsciously, worked to develop similar adaptability and mental agility in others.

In professional life, careers are often thought of as a series of steps, promotions, with increasing responsibility based on experience with a certain set of activities. There is a pathway, a ladder, or whatever metaphor one chooses. It is common to get locked into such a transactional framework of work life, especially in hierarchical organizational settings. I set goals, my boss agrees; I work hard, I meet my goals, I expect to be rewarded with pay increases and/or promotions. When this doesn't happen, it is tempting to react in a similarly transactional way, i.e. "well, fine, I'm going to take it easy next year, take more of my accumulated vacation time," etc. etc.

Imagination offers a way around this deadening approach to work. A robust imagination is particularly useful in overcoming our natural tendencies toward negativity, the so-called negativity bias we discussed in the Introduction. There is plenty of documentation that, when we fail to achieve something, the power of the disappointment is much greater than would have been the sense of accomplishment had we achieved our goal. This bias toward negativity is very strong on the individual level. Disappoint yourself frequently enough and you may never find your way out of the hole you are digging. You need the ability to imagine a better outcome in the future, and a belief in your personal agency to put a new plan into action, the very mental habits that 'Name Withheld' failed to develop.

On the coupledom front, imagination is an essential habit of mind in need of constant investment. When dealing in a partnership, the potential for pessimism increases exponentially without conscious effort. It is, to some extent, a simple numbers game. The 'positive psychologists' who study such matters estimate that our negative sentiments are up to *four* times greater than our positive responses to success (others say 2X, but you get the idea). If so, they note quite seriously, a couple should seek to avoid negative interactions as much as humanly possible. It takes *four* positive interactions to compensate for *one* unhappy interaction, and that is just to keep the scales between happiness and unhappiness in balance, not tilted toward the positive! Just imagine how destructive it is to prolong a conflict over hours or days or to reapply the same failed solutions to a problem area.[29]

Whether you buy into these 'calculations' or not, one thing is clear: such reasoning clearly demonstrates that a relationship is, by definition, a high-risk undertaking. The downside of making a mistake when we invest a high degree of trust in a partner is fraught with danger. At the outset, we can rely on our emotions and physical desire to override our natural risk aversion, and we may unconsciously invest a new relationship with unrealistic, if not unattainable, expectations. The important factor is to recognize what is, or could be, going on and resolve to reset as needed with new ideas and hopes.

---

[29] So-called 'positive' psychologists have developed a variety of ideas and exercises designed to help us overcome our natural tendency toward disappointment. See Susan Shane, "How to Be More Optimistic," *New York Times*, Feb 18, 2020, for a brief summary of such ideas and references, particularly *The Hope Circuit* by Martin Seligman, a pioneer in the positive psychology movement. Shane lists a number of 'exercises' recommended by Seligman to improve optimism. Her sample includes the idea of 'talking back' if you are dealing with a small voice from within that is a downer. Among other ideas: argue with yourself; imagine ideal life in 10 years and write down best possible self in family, in work, in romance; accept disappointment as a reality; look for potential downsides *first* before they hit you unsuspectingly. When you are seeing the worst, imagine the exact opposite, the ideal best, and come to understand that the outcome most likely lies somewhere in the middle! Nothing is ever as good or as bad as it seems. Visualization is another technique with substantial scientific evidence backing its effectiveness for shaping positive forward thinking.

In the case of a couple, imaginative resets are all the more essential to long-term happiness and eventually to the achievement of joyfulness. Every reset is an exercise in psychological flexibility. If you allow your unconscious categories of thought to frame your thinking, you can easily find yourself saying things like "she always complains about that," or "he does that stupid thing (fill in the blank) each time we disagree." Such thinking reflects inflexible categorizing. Such turns of phrase reveal predetermined buckets and no application of imagination.

This is where imagination can come to the rescue with new ideas and new opportunities. A successful long-term relationship requires imaginative 'pivots' in new directions. Nothing ever stays exactly the same and a constant process of 'checking in' with a partner is required to identify mismatched expectations. This is a weekly if not daily process, as finding positive energy in a shared future requires constant reinvention.

A successful pivot builds trust and optimism for both partners. It fosters a shared sense of agency in a couple. No one ever followed a commander up a hill when the commander said he wasn't sure whether they could take the hill. No partner is able to build a life with a partner where disappointment and failure dominate expectations going forward. In a loving relationship, the best medicine is the imaginative and generous partner who shares the problem and *is* the solution. If you are busy being your partner's solution, you will find much less time to let your own negative biases operate! Guaranteed!

You will need to call on your built-in capabilities: your will power, your conscience and your self-awareness, in short your agency, to create a productive reset moment. But commitment and self-analysis will carry you only so far without imagination. Imagination will enable you to see new combinations, new categories, rather than being trapped in past failures. You can mobilize ways of thinking that get beyond the "he said, she said" of daily life. Take a quick glance back at that famous Scott Fitzgerald quote at the beginning of the chapter. It is a brilliant challenge to each one of us. You can dedicate your efforts to being a bigger self for your partner to share, thereby increasing your partner's imaginative upside as well. You will be getting closer and closer to love that doesn't fit easily into any category, but you and your partner will know exactly how undefinable it is! As we look back on these steps, we realize that our multiple transitions were stressful for sure, but we never encountered moments that threatened to disrupt the basic family priorities. Once again the sports metaphor comes to mind. It is possible, in fact essential, to do resets in a marriage, perhaps even multiple times, as long as the pivot foot is solidly anchored. For us, the issue was always what step would bring the most value to our coupledom, to the kids (we were blessed with our daughter when our son turned five), and to the family we were trying to nurture.

There is always something important, and perhaps even better, 'outside the box.' In some ways this attitude can be connected back to our original musings about the nurture of one's 'spirit.' If one is category bound, there are no 'glimpses' of a larger set of possibilities in life, no transcendent possibilities and thus no transcendent love.

Let's end with our best effort to define that undefinable love.

Oh, by the way, the answer to the crossword puzzle clue is 'cereal.' Get it?

CHAPTER TEN

Love Notes

We want to finish the story of 'bis-nonna' and how she orchestrated the search for a potential husband for her daughter, Rosa. The search ended happily despite the many years it took. Claire picks up the story:

> One fine day, a young man from the next town along the coast of the Bay of Naples, Vico Equense, came to dinner at the recommendation of a local priest. He had studied in America—in New York—had become a doctor. Like several of the previous contestants, he was good-looking. Unlike most, however, he was not wealthy, but 'promising' as they used to say. But who knew how he would fare? Rosa presented the tiramisu at the crucial moment. Augusto looked directly into Rosa's eyes and exclaimed, "Meraviglia, ti ringrazie molta, cara Rosa!" Several more specific mentions of flavors and smoothness of the crema promoted Augusto to the next stage of consideration.

Very quickly, Rosa fell in love with this eager suitor. They married three months later (!) and departed immediately for New York where they raised six children (my mother is the youngest) and he practiced medicine for fifty years. They appreciated each other through 52 years of marriage.

By all accounts, Rosa and Augusto shared a lifetime building a reservoir of mutual respect and gratitude. From their brownstone in East Harlem, they delivered medical care and love to the surrounding immigrant community, raised their children, sold War Bonds, attended the Metropolitan Opera, and took great joy in the Italo-American life they invented together.

Rosa and Augusto exemplified transcendent love (for Claire and all who knew them). When the individuals in a couple consistently appreciate one another, and go out of their respective ways to express this appreciation, they create a reservoir of good will, an investment that is built up from such expressions of love and admiration over the years. Not required reassurances in difficult times, but spontaneous and entirely unnecessary reaffirmations of shared happiness. We practice this lesson from Rosa and Augusto on a daily basis. We ask how we can help one another a dozen times a day. We *tell* each other when something the other person says or does makes us happy (or sad). We pay attention and try to remember to express our thoughts just as Bis-nonna demanded of Rosa's suitors.

This idea of investing in efforts that go beyond *quid pro quo* behavior is a key component of this elusive concept of transcendent love. We feel we have built such an endowment of our own through our 'golden moments' described in the chapter on attention. Our endowment operates in a space that is beyond (outside of?... actually we don't know exactly where it operates!) the material dimensions of being. It's out there in the spiritual realm somewhere. It is not subject to the transactional universe of reason, time, and physical change.

Without an activated spirit, you cannot grasp or appreciate transcendence, and partnership life can simply drift into living a series of transactions, expenditures rather than investments. This is not so much a physical or moral failing as it is simply a suboptimal use of your (shared) human potential. You need to keep investing in a loving relationship. It needs to continue to grow or it will begin to wither. There is no 'stasis' in which love simply stands still.

This was the special gift of Bis-nonna to her daughter and son-in-law. Even in her day, she saw beyond the transactional dimensions of the coupling process. Yes, religious training, family traditions and financial assets were a consideration then as now (and maybe even more so in those days). We have nothing against hard work and material progress. Ambition and entrepreneurial energy are essential to deal effectively with the material world. But Bis-nonna understood the danger of treating a wedding as a transaction. This is not a rational, self-optimizing business deal. It is a spiritual union that cannot flourish as a 'one plus one equals two' proposition. It absolutely requires the intangibles of admiration and appreciation to have any chance of success over time.

Our coupledom endowment also offsets the dangers of self-deception. Consider something as seemingly positive as a personal or family celebration. When a couple inevitably loses the hormonal high of the falling in love period (over weeks, months, and perhaps years), one solution may be to turn the 'pursuit of happiness' into a full-time quest. Relying on a continuous stream of celebrations to activate pleasurable feelings is not, however, a sustainable pathway to 'real' love. It is exhausting psychologically to sustain happiness through unending economic progress, and it is likewise exhausting to invent the next celebration to preserve the feeling of celebrating:

> American culture insists that we run at breathless pace from sugar-laced celebration to celebration… Christmas, New Years, Mardi Gras, Valentine's Day, Fourth of July, and on and on… But life is not a Disney Cruise.[30]

While the writer may sound a bit like a scold here, we think her Disney reference is spot on. We meet people who constantly over-program themselves day after day, week after week and complain about how busy they are. We don't mean the kind of busy that affects working parents who deal with transaction overload every day and can only hope for a fifteen minute bathroom break. We mean folks who go to great lengths to avoid doing nothing, even for a few minutes. Claire's sister nicknamed a friend of hers 'sharky' because of her apparent need for constant movement to stay alive.

'Keeping busy' may be more than an addiction to transactions. It is a perfect cover for self-deception. It might be a symptom of some level of unhappiness with your self, of not liking your self well enough to want to spend time with your self. Perhaps it reveals a deficit in self-worth or self-confidence that is essential to constructive partnering. Such an exercise in self-deception is easy to miss. A shared endowment of golden moments can insure your transaction/transcendence equilibrium. Everyone should be willing to adopt a skeptical posture concerning their

---

[30] Tish Harrison Warren, "Face the Darkness: How I Fell in Love with Advent," *New York Times*, November 30, 2019. Warren is an Anglican priest and author of *Everyday Spirituality.*

own convictions and motives. Assuming you are absolutely right about matters of mind or spirit often betrays a naïve level of self-understanding.

Speaking of subtlety, we cannot resist passing along another bit of wisdom from C.S. Lewis concerning self-deception. He suggests that the word 'unselfish' has come to represent an idealized behavior, the kind of mindset that eager people seek in their partners. But Lewis points out that this term implies a transactional mindset. Any terms that include the 'self' such as self-sacrifice, self-discipline, or selflessness imply the idea of giving and getting. I give up 'x' and I get, by implication, 'y' in return. To put it a bit more aggressively, self-denial is *not* a good basis for the attainment of love. Any counting or scorecard keeping is the antithesis of the goal of becoming a shared self with a partner. So one should be wary of the power of language to (mis)-categorize.

Lewis recommends that the word 'charity' replace unselfishness as the desirable trait to be cultivated with a partner. Charity is not passive or transactional. In its purest state, it is proactive and other-oriented. There is no *quid pro quo*, no expectation of a personal return on the gift/investment. There is no finite self in any part of the equation. [31] There is an expanded self that is liberated from the 'gator brain' and from finite logic. The giver's happiness is expanded by the improved fortunes of the other. We are getting closer to a state of mind in which we can generate a 'loving' relationship, one in which two selves build an expanded and liberated shared self.

One additional observation concerning the positive value of a

---

[31] These ideas are very much aligned with the Jewish laws of charity (tzedakah) as outlined by the twelfth-century scholar Maimonides. The ideal giver is invisible to the recipient and others. An excellent example of organized religion's "wisdom tradition."

couple's shared endowment: it can provide energy for difficult moments and decisions. Remember our discussions of pivots and resets? The metaphorical journey to and through coupledom includes dead ends, detours, and just plain getting lost. It is not an interstate highway trip from point A to point B. It is essential to get used to this way of operating, to remain patient, to keep checking the GPS. In difficult times, the power of agency will be tested. Can a positive direction be found when really bad things happen? When you are blocked, unable to invent a new way forward, you can call on a reservoir of shared moments, of inspiring glimpses into transcendent reality to energize your reset. It is often hard work to create positive meaning from difficult events that impact your partnership. A couple will always need a power source for a sustained, transcendent loving relationship and an endowment of shared glimpses of a larger reality can provide just that.

Transactionally-dominated couples will struggle with the many challenges to their relationship that cannot be quantified, or rationalized, or described coherently in reasoned language. Yet this non-rational 'stuff' has the power to make or break their relationship. The spiritual dimension of coupledom is not managed through use of the rules of logic that operate your rational mind. As we discussed in the chapter on imagination, everyone's thinking is limited by the categories into which all of us (unconsciously) sort ideas. In the spiritual domain, however, these buckets do not define us. Categories can be dissolved into new formulations that may seem paradoxical on the surface. Scott Fitzgerald goes even farther in his famous quotation cited at the beginning of the chapter on imagination, asserting that 'first class minds' in general have the fluidity and 'agency' to hold competing ideas simultaneously without becoming paralyzed. This is not our 'reason' in action.

We have reflected on three testing 'resets' from our fifty plus year coupledom. We are well aware of how fortunate we have been to avoid facing genuine tragedies. We have never gone hungry. We have never lost a child. We have never been near a war zone. Our challenges have been modest in the greater scheme of things. But our core values have been tested on a few occasions and our investments in coupledom have served us well in these difficult moments. Every couple will inevitably be challenged whether by events of their own making or simply by the fickle finger of fate. The challenge is to make such occurrences a source of strength, rather than permanent conflict, in your coupledom.

RESET I

We have already mentioned the first challenge our partnership faced—our dual careers. The most difficult such moment occurred early in our careers. Following the shared Living Learning Center project, we struck out in new directions. Claire became an assistant professor of French at Purdue University and David a member of the IU central administration overseeing new degree programs for adult learners. A home base in Indianapolis kept the family together. Three years later we were ready for greener pastures and Claire once again scored two giant steps on the traditional academic ladder. She received a fellowship for a year of research at the National Humanities Center, a think tank in North Carolina, as well as a tenure track professorship (i.e. one leading to a permanent faculty position) at Emory University in Atlanta to follow the completion of her fellowship. Accepting the fellowship was a no-brainer and David dutifully found work as a lecturer in French at nearby North Carolina State for the fellowship year. Things got tougher, however, when, during that year, he was offered a deanship at the University of Pennsylvania School of Arts and Sciences. It was an either/or moment. Ivy league or Emory? Pursuit of tenure or administrative work?

Atlanta or Philly? One or the other of us would become the 'trailing spouse.'

Claire felt it was only fair, given that David had followed her to North Carolina, for him to accept the deanship. But it is difficult to convey the sacrifice required to turn down her rare professorial opportunity at a major university. This was the successful culmination of a decade of professional preparation in a tightly controlled field of expertise. It seemed unlikely that another such opportunity would present itself in the future.

Friends encouraged us to each take the offered positions and 'test' which setting proved best for a year or two. But that was a non-starter. The family would stick together, and Claire, fresh from the prestige of working with distinguished scholars from across the globe, chose to head to Penn without colleagues, without income, and without 'standing,' as the French might say. She faced the house hunting, the complexity of inner-city school options for the kids, and her professional isolation with remarkable poise. The family never missed a beat. At her best in a crisis, Claire's entrepreneurial skills again came to the fore, as with the LLC, and soon she had built a mini-empire of foreign language pedagogy programs with funds raised entirely by her creative appeals to private foundations. She became the go-to consultant for foreign language departments at the National Endowment for the Humanities and published a widely-used book on the management of foreign-language departments in higher education. Eventually even Penn noticed such overlooked talent on campus and Claire joined the founding faculty of the Joseph Lauder Institute, a joint effort of the Wharton School of Business and the School of Arts and Sciences offering an international MBA/MA.

In a few short years, eight to be exact, Claire had transformed her professional profile from scholar to academic thought leader. A career filled with honorary degrees, board appointments, global travels, financial rewards and notoriety followed. But it would be a mistake to overlook the courage required to give up her dream of a professorship in the interest of the family.

RESET II

In later years, we faced another serious challenge that once again tested our spiritual reserves. David met 'another woman,' and conveniently (gutlessly) failed to tell Claire. Of course she found out (after the affair had ended) and was forced to face David's self-indulgent weakness. This was uncharted water for our relationship.

David had basically destroyed the credibility and respect he had earned over decades of partnership. Clearly the ability to apologize with sincerity had been lost and a certain sense of helplessness ensued. Coupledom, the framework of shared trust in which we had been operating, had collapsed and it was difficult to know where to turn. Claire reflects on this sad period:

> The experience was disorienting for both of us. During our separation that I imposed upon the discovery of David's affair, I got some counseling from a professional psychologist. She encouraged me to see that, given my contributions as wife, mother and wage earner, I did not deserve this disloyalty and disrespect. She was a brilliant woman, but I gradually began to see how she was leading me through a transactional analysis of my situation. I had done these things, therefore, I deserved this kind of response. This for that. Makes great sense... really logical... very normal

and personally supportive advice to contemporary women and modern marriages.

I certainly felt wronged and disrespected, but I was trying to figure out what to *do* about the situation. I realized that I had to make my response fit all the dimensions of my life, my marriage, my physical, mental and spiritual life.

Divorce?? That would mean no role for forgiveness... but what about the "forgiveness" I had been taught as part of preparing for the sacrament of Confession? My children knew that. What would be the lesson my actions would teach them if they knew their Dad was sorry the affair happened and wanted to re-promise our commitment to each other? Actually, as I was struggling, our daughter reminded me that I had promised only death would part us, not a single mistake. Hmm-m-m, true. I also realized that I had experienced God's forgiveness of my mistakes when I asked for forgiveness in Confession. Was I not called to offer forgiveness to others?? Yes, my body and mind felt devastated, my spirit was disappointed, but the more I let my spirit lead me, the more clearly I could see that I, even we as a couple, had never been led first by mind and body. We had always kept our spirits in the lead.

So after some experimentation of my own, I understood that the real me could not tolerate a divorce or another man. David and I had built a transcendent unit in a love that, like anything human, was imperfect and subject to serious mistakes. It still featured the commitment to 'staying together,' the power of resets, despite career distractions and even an affair.

After a lengthy separation, I agreed to move back to living together, initially only in the same two-bedroom apartment, not the same bed. I cried every day for almost six months, still so broken-hearted. But David's apology and gentle, imaginative efforts to win me back became more powerful and convincing each day. I prayed for strength and full re-commitment to my marriage oath and to trust. My forgiveness had to become firm and real. Day by day we practiced talking about how we had fallen in love, how we had studied together, traveled together and parented together. We moved fully, lovingly back in together.

The endowment of trust and 'charity' was badly damaged by David's selfishness. And yet in the end it was the endowment that provided the resources needed to 'stop the bleeding' and invent a way forward. In our own moment of truth and reconciliation, we were able to get beyond the transactional anger and disappointment. David was able to own up to the hurtfulness of his self-indulgence and to ask for forgiveness with sincerity. Claire, with her practiced reconciliation, forgave. Such generosity of spirit gave agency to a difficult reset. We defined a way forward that made this episode a part of our lives, not a forbidden topic of conversation or a weapon to be wielded in moments of conflict. We strengthened our shared reality and our trust as we reaffirmed what mattered most to both of us.

RESET III

Years later, following "retirement" from our day jobs, we re-invented our professional selves once again. We launched Gaudiani Associates, our family business dedicated to research, writing, speaking and consulting on the role of philanthropy in the American economy. It was exciting and satisfying work with speaking engagements and consults across the country and in several European countries as well. It was energizing to work together again, as we had back in the days of the Living Learning Center, after decades with separate careers.

During these years, Claire faced a variety of physical challenges including the gradual loss of nerve service on the right side of her body. The ensuing weakness made walking and writing a never-ending challenge. She persevered, of course, working with trainers and physical therapists to maintain functionality (and she still does), but fate piled on an assortment of additional auto-immune diseases, blood disorders, and eventually the hemorrhagic stroke that we mentioned in the chapter on humor (the stroke itself was no joke!). She has recovered with no permanent damage to her speech or mental capacities, but the lengthy rehabilitation set back her hard-earned progress in overcoming the right side weakness. Her patience has been severely tested as she has been obliged to give up much of her physical independence. No driving, no solo travel, in fact not a lot of solo anything.

Care-giving has seemed natural and seamless for David, despite the impact on his independence. It requires focus and attention 24/7 to ensure the safety and comfort of a partner whose capacity for self-care has been damaged. The 'patient' must make endless sacrifices of privacy, independence and agency. It is constantly stressful to struggle with a balky body. And a caregiver must search for the right balance between too much 'hovering' and too little support at a crucial moment. Perhaps the biggest adjustment for caregiving is patience, for life slows down to a remarkable degree. Happily, we have achieved a satisfying balance of these many variables and we have our shared humor, attention and imagination to thank for these successes.

Each of these three resets, in different ways, has tested our shared agency. No one has the power to control all the events of life. Lots of people do live with the illusion that they are, in fact, in control of what happens. They take credit when things go well and usually find someone else to blame when things go badly. Much better to acknowledge that, from the get-go, the best laid plans can and will go off the tracks. The fickle finger will sometimes intervene to disrupt the most careful thinking. On other occasions, as in the case of David's infidelity, the disruption is self-inflicted. The solution is not to despair or to stop putting one's best effort into thoughtful planning, but to cultivate your collective capacity to control (or at least manage) the *meaning* of what happens.

Agency generates the story of your life in partnership. It is the power that erases victimhood, no matter how cruel or unjust events may be. It is a product of the partnership's shared self-awareness, which ensures against self-deception. It is also a product of a couple's shared consciousness, that ability to 'see' themselves in action, to evaluate their shared trust, appreciation and communication, and to course correct when such analyses reveal gaps or flaws in the loving relationship. We have chosen to overcome our conflicts and shortcomings by integrating them into a larger context. Our commitments have enabled us to blend our physical interdependence into a seamless way of being. We are grateful for facing challenges that we have found the power to overcome. Our story is not a tale of gradual loss marked by the ravages of time. Life is short and then you die, right? Yes we do live in time, at least our bodies do, as we can attest, and neither of us looks exactly like we did on our wedding day. But... so what? We know we are more alive, engaged, appreciative, joyful and in love than we were in the days of yearbook photos and rock and roll. (As you might guess, Claire never actually rocked or rolled much in those days, but she has since embraced the music of another Michigan guy, Bob Seger. Check out his classic anthem "Night Moves" if you don't know it.)

It may seem paradoxical to stress how important self-love is as a building block for our love. But in our way of seeing things, you are not on a mission to dissolve your 'self' as you somehow disappear into a mysterious merged being with your partner. We see no particular merit in dramatic injunctions to obliterate one's identity in the service of larger forces, cosmic or otherwise. On the contrary, you need to bring a 'best version of yourself' to coupledom. And that includes, for sure, attention paid to your own self, the person who is most difficult for you to understand. Just think of the many examples of self-deception we have noted (including David's egregious behavior) throughout this text. Coupledom should enable you to expand your self as you become more secure and more energized in a loving partnership. You should find comfort, control and the courage to recognize your own shortcomings, as well as appropriate pride in your abilities and accomplishments. It doesn't all have to be totally accurate or totally rationale. We all have our quirks, fears and blind spots. But you must know yourself well enough to draw on your 'assets'—imagination/humor/attention—in a spirit of humility. Humility signals permeability, an openness to, and appreciation of, the other, and to the possibilities of life in general. No loving partnership will function without humility.

In conclusion, we want to talk a bit about this idea of an expanded, perhaps even boundless, loving self. Throughout our musings, we are aware that we have talked almost exclusively about the self and a partner. This has been intentional because we believe a couple must absolutely rely on one another in the creation of their partnership. Advice from a third party may be fine, but no third party can constitute a meaningful element of a loving couple, not parents, or children, or friends, or anyone else, not even the dog! However, the joy of a loving partnership can and should be shared with others. Joyfulness, as we understand it, is not finite or unstable. Our supply cannot be diminished no matter how much we share. In fact, joyfulness creates a kind of imperative to extend ourselves as much as possible.[32]

Christianity puts forward the idea that God *is* love... infinite, incomprehensible, and unwavering, but kind and forgiving. Those who love God seek to expand their being through communion with Him. Moreover, such a possibility is always on offer, no matter one's personal failings or poor track record. Love God and He will love you back because He already loves you. You just hadn't noticed! The door is always open, as the prodigal son discovered, and joy is the reward.

This powerful, if improbable, concept holds great value. It is not necessary to interpret the idea literally to appreciate its power. An activated, spiritual self can grasp what is beyond the rational understanding of a finite, transactional self. Happily (or rather, joyfully)

---

[32] You may notice that we are here deploying a word that is omnipresent in Christian vocabulary, not because we feel that religious faith is the only source of 'joy,' but on the contrary, because we believe that the gift of joyfulness is available to those who find real love. David grew up playing the piano and organ for his church Sunday school. Virtually all the hymns either celebrated victory ("Onward Christian Soldiers," "The Fight is On! Sound the Battle Cry!") or joy ("Joy-Bells Ringing in Your Heart," "Joy to the World," "Let the Joy Overflow"). These latter hymns were, of course, celebrating coming to know the love of Jesus. But, without blasphemy, it is difficult to find a better word for the feeling of transcendent love in a broader sense.

if one has glimpsed 'infinite' love in a transcendent partnership, it is possible to imagine just such an interpretation of divine presence. It is also possible to understand, in a concrete way, the concept of 'loving thy neighbor.' It makes perfect sense to encompass as many others as possible in an extended circle of optimistic agency.

We first embrace, naturally enough, the 'others' we already 'love,' not as we love each other, but those closest to us in body, mind and spirit such as parents, children, siblings and grandchildren. We have more than enough savings in our spiritual accounts to share our optimism and joyfulness with our one remaining parent (whom you have heard about), our two children, and our five grandchildren. Claire's mother is, as noted, an independent and strong woman, but Claire speaks with her by phone for an hour or two each day. Our children and their kids are all on their own journeys, dealing with the plans and pivots, the accomplishments and the disappointments that come with the territory. We consider it a major component of our own happiness that we speak or text with both of our kids and at least one or two of the grandkids on a daily basis. We value the close contact very deeply, and sometimes remain a bit amazed that we can still function as a sounding board and occasionally contribute a bit of advice, practical or otherwise, to their well-being.

We hope that they feel some overflow of our joyfulness as a couple and sense that, at least for now, we have the resources to manage ourselves and plenty left to give to others. Our family is confident in and through us and this outcome is a direct product of our transcendent love for each other. We also endeavor to care for and about people outside our immediate family. It is a cliché to discuss the life of a teacher in terms of 'generosity' to one's students, but we have spent a lifetime attempting to practice this virtue in classrooms and office hours. As you may have noticed, Claire definitely had a head start on a lot of the most important ideas that got us to where we are today. David has come to understand one way that Claire's boundless self has manifested itself in the lives of others:

> What is the special sauce that wins teaching awards at just about every institution where you have taught? From French 101 at Indiana University to the Economics of Philanthropy at New York University almost 50 years later. Finally I get it… after all these years. It is because you have always treated every student in front of you as a whole person, not just as a 'mind' to be trained. Whether the students knew it or not, you assumed they were there to invest in their minds *and* their spirits, *and*, given the frequent advice they got on cooking and nutrition, in their bodies as well. Maybe this explains why you still hear directly from dozens of them thirty and forty years later.

> I remember the course you invented at Conn College called "Literature, Service and Social Reflection." Students read *The Bluest Eye*, *The Invisible Man*, and similar classics while simultaneously volunteering in the public schools and community centers of New London, CT. They kept diaries and used their 'experiential' learning to analyze their reading assignments. You understood the importance of learning to 'see yourself in the other,' before other folks woke up. Students engaged literature with their minds and their spirits.

> You had been fortunate to study with faculty members at Conn as an undergraduate who

shared this perspective, i.e. that study of the humanities deals with both rational and spiritual dimensions of self. But by the time you became president of Conn some 25 years later, the faculty perspective seemed changed. When you spoke openly about moral imperatives, about 'what do you do with what you know?' some colleagues were uncomfortable. A different paradigm had evolved which might best be characterized as "embrace the subject matter and invite interested students to study it."

Yet your awards, voted by students over the years, reveal the enthusiasm with which they greeted your embrace of them as people, rather than brains encased in bodies. They probably couldn't say it, but they intuited that your classroom was different because you recognized and indeed urged them to cultivate all dimensions of themselves, not just their rational facilities. Every learning event was a chance to think about your purpose in life, your 'self' in all its dimensions. Remember when you taught Racine's *Phaedra,* one of your favorite dramas of all time, to undergrads at Purdue? And a student piped up "But I don't get it. Why was she so upset? She didn't even sleep with him!?"

There is a 'humanities' teaching moment big enough to drive a truck through, thanks to a carefully taught seventeenth-century play about some Greek demigods. You didn't just give the students your knowledge; you gave them a chunk of themselves. Now that is worth the tuition.

When we get onto the topic of loving your neighbor, we are inevitably reminded of the idealism underlying the founding of our nation, a topic we have studied in conjunction with our books about the origins and economic impact of philanthropy. The United States is the only nation on earth founded on a creed, as G.K. Chesterton pointed out. But long before the Declaration of Independence was drafted, we have that famous sermon delivered on the good ship *Arabella* by John Winthrop, who would become governor of the Massachusetts Bay Colony in the mid 1600s. He wrote, "in this new land, we must work as one man, and those of us with superfluities must share, until all have met their necessities." This was not a zero sum proposition nor a win-lose 'transaction' (although Winthrop was a pretty good businessman who had financed the trip to the new world by selling shares in a 'fur trading company' he planned to create). It was an idealistic, transcendent vision of 'the greater good,' of loving thy neighbor as thyself. We understand the idea that, as we enjoy the privilege of learning, freely, about ourselves and others, we face a moral imperative to *do* something with what we know, and that is to help as many of our fellow citizens as possible to share the joy of love over a lifetime. We hope we have a few more years to get better at this project.

APPENDICES

APPENDIX I

Our Response To Name Withheld

Letter repeated for convenience

I'm nearly 40 and I find myself at a crossroads that feels more like a dead end... I've spent much of my life and thought and income in pursuit of beauty in one form or another: design, fashion, the beauty or 'wellness' industries. This is very much a professional hazard: my career in glossy magazines and advertising as a photo editor is all about making beautiful images of beautiful things that I've selected look even more beautiful. Often, when I think how much of my time I've devoted to my own appearance or to matters of aesthetics I cringe, though I've often been the person in any given room defending things like style and design from accusations of superficiality and frivolity.

There's a clear irony here, given how much thought I've put into what things—art, interiors, people—should look like, that I've come to a place in which I no longer know what my own life should look like. I literally do not know what to do with myself and what I should believe in anymore... I've lost my sense of meaning to myself... I feel like the culture has moved on without me and I don't know what to do.

I feel alone in many ways... and unsuccessful by most measures. I don't own a home and no one needs me. I am nobody's mother or child. My friends and peers have gone on to have families, to marry and stop working... I'm kind of astonished when I see how many of my peers, educated, once ambitious women friends don't work professionally anymore. They've given up.

I don't entirely envy them, but still... I'm not sure where this leaves me, though I am accountable to no one but myself. On good days, I can take a yoga class and still feel like life's potential is still just around the corner if I'm just open to it; on bad ones, I feel such futility, like I've squandered my own youth and beauty in the hall of mirrors that is our consumerist society. Am I simply being solipsistic here? Or is this what getting older is about, acknowledging one's comedown to the brutal reality of life?—

"Name Withheld"

Wow! what an outpouring of sadness, if not downright despair. Clearly the first remedy called for is a large hug and a lot of reassurance that everything will be OK. But hugs are difficult to dispense over distance, so we will need to rely on some warm words of encouragement instead. We have divided our response into two parts. David, the more analytically-oriented part of our shared self, has done the diagnosis of Name's issues. Claire, the forceful problem-solver, has taken charge of recommending what 'Name' should *do* to escape this 'dark night of the soul.'

David: Name's Problems

'Name Withheld' finds herself in an echo chamber of her own making. She is indicting herself and convicting herself in the same breath. She appears helpless and victimhood is looming. She has lost control of everything, including the future. She is disconnected from any external sources of perspective, guidance, or encouragement. Her energy and optimism are non-existent. Her 'assets,' as implied in the letter, such as education, writing skills, good health and some financial security, are not being mobilized for her benefit.

Name's deep isolation is based on a couple of classic errors. She has counted on her job/career to produce meaning and purpose in her life. This is a confusion of 'success,' as measured by job title, promotions, salary, and so on, with 'happiness' or satisfaction. Work life is an important contributor to a sense of self-worth, but it quickly becomes a series of tasks: meet the next deadline, get the next promotion, get the next whatever. That kind of 'rat race' overshadows the need for reflection, self-analysis and resets. It overwhelms the human gifts of free will, self-consciousness and conscience. Name has been thinking and acting the same way over a twenty year career. But time and ideas do march on and Name has missed the boat.

Secondly, Name freely admits that her mode of operation has been as a solo actor. There are no teammates to be found, no coalitions built, no partnerships developed. She paints herself as the frequent lone champion of the aesthetic perspective. She has, sadly, become a self-pitying martyr to the cause.

As a result of these errors, she has not nurtured the part of her 'self' that might enable her to grow and change. She has cared for her body (she mentions yoga and "attending to her appearance"). She has invested in her mind (well-educated, writes well, etc.), but completely ignored her spirit. She is a prototype, a case study, of spiritual neglect. In fact she is so captured by the material world that she now fears aging (at the ripe old age of 40!) is producing only decline and decay!

This circumstance is particularly ironic, because Name has chosen the most spiritual of ideas, beauty, as her professional calling and daily preoccupation. Beauty, after all, is a quality that defies the limits of rationality. It is a window into the possibilities of transcendence. It is an eternal ideal that does not degrade with time. But the spiritual quality of beauty, its ability to provoke glimpses of a reality that is more than material, real but undefinable, is no longer accessible to Name. I suspect that it was, once upon a time, but that dimension of beauty has been erased, or at least corrupted, by the "hall of mirrors that is our consumerist society." Now beauty has become a commodity controlled by 'tastemakers,' and available to be bought and sold by the 'one percenters' among her friends who married rich guys and went off to live in exotic places. Name has ended up with the worst of both worlds: she does not have the wherewithal to own beautiful things and now her aesthetic sensibility has been paralyzed by her failures to invest in her own spiritual agency. So what is to be done???

Claire's recommendations for 'Name'

I would lovingly suggest that Name embark on an emergency search for her personal agency. Her core values, her anchors in a changing world, are missing in action and she must do some serious 'excavating' to re-find what matters to her. What she must *not* do is risk repeating the errors that led her to this 'dark night' by jumping into a new job or a new location or a new relationship.

Re-finding oneself is no simple matter but it can be done. This will require a reset and a reset requires a pivot foot firmly anchored in core values. Finding those values is job #1. She must reawaken her spirit, that part of her self where joyfulness, energy and indeed a grasp of 'beauty' can be found. Only then can Name experiment with new ideas and new 'moves' with the other foot. As long as the pivot foot is set, she can test and retest while staying true to her self.

Her revitalization effort should start with a version of an 'examination of conscience.' That is, she should find a quiet place, leave her technology behind and ask her *self* a few questions:

• What actions or activities do improve her mood and encourage her optimism?
• Does she ever give her full attention to something that brings her personal delight and involves no transactions, (no this-for-that exchange of her effort in order to earn something??)

If most answers are "no," she should promise some time each day to develop a relationship, even a real partnership with her *self*. I mean cultivate the links between body care and mind care with care of her spirit. We do have one clue. Name mentions that her yoga sessions bring her at least a passing sense of optimism. This activity would seem to offer an answer to question three above. Making this simple investment in her physical well-being is helpful.

She should clearly build on this idea of self care and extend it to her spirit. She might, for instance, start with a quiet reading of some accessible poetry… Frost's "Road Less Traveled," for instance, or better yet, why not *The Little Prince*, a masterpiece of accessible, imaginative inspiration for anyone's spirit? Maybe she thinks about roads in her own life or how her own imagination might work as well as the Prince's does! Maybe she tries reading some pages of Victor Frankl's *Man's Search for Meaning*. She focuses on his mind, his body, his spirit. What could he be like?? Her options for inspiration are endless.

Since Name is clearly visually-oriented, she could choose a favorite object to concentrate on. But here the danger is that her 'professional hazard baggage' might interfere. But she must engage *without* her professional baggage. Whether poetry or painting, music or stories, she should deploy her full attention and focus on her reactions without judgment… no critical expertise, no right or wrong, or cool or woke analysis needed now… She must seek a holistic unmediated reaction. For instance, with a few deep breaths and sustained attention on the poem or the art, does she sense wonder? Awe? Admiration? Timelessness? Probably not, at least not the first time, given her current condition, but she must persevere.

Name could also try to reawaken her spirit by engaging with another person who is more 'alive' to possibilities, more engaged with the multiplicity of options in her environment. Someone she knows, knew or learned about through reading a biography. Regardless, the idea is that Name get comfortable, see the individual in her mind's eye and imagine, or have, a short, involved conversation. When the back and forth is over, it is time to reflect on what feels new; questions like "What did I learn about myself? About her/him/them? Why did I choose this person? Do I need more contacts with real persons like this one?" Each of these private, short encounters engages the whole *self* and helps a person to grow optimism, self-confidence, and trust in oneself.

I even have a suggestion for a person for 'Name Withheld' to meet. I'll make an introduction right here and look into getting them together. I know a 99-year-old woman who is still leading a strong productive, healthy life *full of meaning to herself and others*. She always worked out in a gym, still does so today three times a week, so she has kept a strong body. She always read widely, and both attended and taught classes, so she kept a strong mind. But unlike Name, she pursued an equally strong spiritual life. Her universe is larger than the material, physical world and she connects her body and mind with the life and energy of her spiritual world every day. Egad, she prays!

She visits sick elderly people in her retirement village three or four times a week. Most she doesn't even know; many are in deep memory loss. She stays in loving contact with grand and great grand kids, nieces, nephews, and friends of all ages. She contributes to people in need, especially immigrant families, from her very modest widow's pension. Her spirit of loving her neighbor is active in her everyday life.

The result of daily integration of three areas of commitment is that all her human parts – body, mind, spirit - were all tended, challenged, engaged all through her life. In 1923 when she was born, that seemed like the norm. If anything there was more attention on the spirit than on body care or continuing education. Today, the reverse seems to be the case.

Most of Name's peers with whom I am acquainted are uncomfortable about spirituality of any kind. Some are even edgy about facing the idea that in addition to their bodies and minds that they do tend, they also have spirits that they mostly ignore.

For our 99-year-old, the harmony she maintained around her body, mind, *and* spirit may be the reason she has the same joyful personality at 99 that she had, according to family, friends and colleagues, at 29, 49, 69 and 89. OK, so one fine day at 97 years old, she woke up from a nap and felt a sudden, severe pain in her remaining functioning eye (very common macular degeneration and complications had ruined the other eye years ago). When she stood up, she realized she could barely see at all. She called the clinic in her retirement village. During the ten minutes they needed to get to her apartment, she watched her remaining whispers of light and colors blacken over.

An optical vein had broken in her remaining eye and made her totally blind in both eyes within an hour of the sudden pain. Many doctors prepared her family for her depression, disinterest in life, and collapse of her energetic personality. Not inevitable, they said, but not unlikely. For two weeks, frequent panic attacks, confusion and grief overwhelmed her. She prayed for strength and patience each day, but her physical being was under assault. Her brain, losing the masses of minute-by-minute data input from her eyes, was disoriented.

It took a full two weeks of skilled medical care daily for her blood pressure to re-normalize and her panic attacks to subside. The predicted depression, loss of normal personality, feelings of despair, and loss of purpose never happened. She did lose her sense of taste and smell for some weeks. She also lost her appetite. All these deficits gradually returned when she got home to her apartment.

With aides to help 24/7, she got her home-cooked food she could smell cooking. She could listen to the news, her Audible books, and favorite music. She could take phone calls and welcome visitors. All of it, even the fragrance of big fresh lilies, re-linked her senses, her body, and mind, to life and joy. At the end of the first month, she asked for help to walk to the gym so she could resume her work-outs. She also wanted to be walked to the clinic where she could visit the Alzheimer's patients she had visited before her hemorrhage. She began therapy to learn to use a white cane and get around on her own. She returned even more seriously to her Audible book list and went through Michelle Obama's and Sonia Sotomayor's autobiographies in one week. She was eager to discuss each at length with visitors. She went from 24 to 10 hours of aide-care a day, confident to be alone in her blindness.

I will stop. I think my message is out there. 'Name Withheld' is wrong to blame (old) age as the reason for feeling that she has "lost her meaning to herself." She is right, however, to share her feelings. They are a problem to her well-being. I think that maybe, just maybe, the 99-year-old will convey an even bigger lesson than that getting older doesn't necessarily doom people to sadness and grim, lonely self-reflections. Maybe the 99-year-old is living, not speaking, her advice to Name and to the rest of us as well.

Security and optimism in her long life come from engaging all dimensions of the self. Meaning in life remains constant and clear as a result of tending *her full self.* So, whatever happens in life, even a crisis, she still knows what life should look like, and what she loves and believes in. She illustrates what it takes to build and sustain the powers needed to sustain her joy for herself and for others.

APPENDIX II

Claire On Teaching Confirmation Classes Today

For the past five years, I have been teaching Confirmation class! My very diverse classes include ten to sixteen young teens who attend all kinds of schools from very best to worst that are available in NYC. The curriculum is focused on Catholic teaching about Christ's Gospel of love, and how these young people can become 'the best version of themselves' as God hopes they will. In short, I find myself teaching the concepts that Sister Regis and Father Duncan helped me discover more than 50 years ago.

How does this work in class? One recent session offered the students three 'scenarios' to discuss. One showed Alex at his desk struggling over whether to focus on his mid-term English essay due tomorrow or leave it for later and play on-line games with his buddies. Question: What would you do if you were in Alex's shoes? Another showed Samantha approaching the subway station turnstile as her friends call out, "Come on, Sam, we jumped! Hurry up, jump, Sam!" Question: What would you do if you were in Sam's shoes? The third shows Carl vlogging with his friends. His brother walks by. Carl says "Tom, all the kids are giving this noob such a bad time, making fun of him, taking all his stuff. Glad I'm not a noob anymore." Tom says, "You should be able to help him, Carl..." "I know, but I'm afraid..." says Carl. Question: What would you do if you were in Carl's shoes?

Students launch into an animated set of answers. They identify the "problem" in each scenario. Alex's procrastination links to personal experiences of several kids. They offer thoughtful conclusions about how they deal with procrastination. They cite Samantha's peer pressure to do something illegal, immoral, or just dopey. One student even remarks that Samantha should change her friend group! (Great idea!) Carl inspires the students to react against cyberbullying. They agree it is hard. Bullies can turn on defenders of the weak. But the students come up with ways to act that enable Carl to build toward becoming a better version of himself. Several kids share a personal event and how they dealt with it.

After all their thoughtful interactions, it is easy to name the strengths they have at their disposal:

1. They each have a conscience, the power to determine right from wrong.

2. They each have self-awareness. They can see themselves acting in their lives.

3. They each have free will. They can and must take responsibility for their own actions.

Sound familiar? We conclude by showing that these three powers, working together, create Agency. The power each person has to perform independently and responsibly as the pilot, the captain, of her/his own ship... the agent in charge of decisions that shape a life and a character. Of course, we stress that these are gifts from God. These gifts come with lots of help, inspiration from the Spirit of God, so individuals can become, over time, the best versions of themselves. Young people want power and freedom. They respond with genuine enthusiasm to the class. They have practiced how to remain aware and in charge.

APPENDIX III

David On A Very Brief History Of Western Beauty

Take a moment to reread the brief passage from William Wordsworth's poem cited at the beginning of Chapter Seven on attention. The crisis of 'society vs nature' invoked by Wordsworth's poem generated much discussion about beauty as a category of human experience. Up to his time, beauty was mostly defined in 'classical' terms that had originated with the Greeks and Romans. It relied heavily on the notion of idealized forms, whether in architecture, poetry or the human body. Beauty consisted of objects or compositions that were representational, balanced, symmetrical, and carefully constructed/controlled. Classicists offer the inspiring power of rational perfection to invoke a form of beauty that presents itself as timeless, outside the ravages of time despite its material form. Beauty, in a sense, was a humanly created form of immortality. Think of the Parthenon, the Arc de Triomphe, the Lincoln Memorial, statues of Greek and Roman gods, the formalism of an Horatian ode. This form of beauty continues to evoke a glimpse of transcendence.

In the decades before Wordsworth penned his poem, a number of thinkers began to offer alternative forms of beauty. They found their ideas through connections with nature. They were inspired by the seemingly 'wild' and chaotic, undomesticated and unbuilt world. They found their glimpses of awesome transcendence in thunderstorms and waterfalls or butterflies and wild orchids. They interpreted their emotional responses as signals of a different kind of beauty, something more provocative, turbulent and stimulating to the 'sentiments' than the reasoned perfection of Leonardo's famous Vitruvian Man. Remember those novels you never read... Rousseau: *La Nouvelle Heloise*, Sterne: *A Sentimental Journey* and maybe the one you did read... *The Sorrows of Young Werther* by Goethe (the Faust guy)? These works and countless others proposed a different way of encountering 'the beautiful.'

In many ways, the conflation of beauty with strong emotions would seem to signal a step back from the 'transcendent.' After all, emotions are part of our material selves. They are not part of a spiritual world of ideals and perfection. But the 'sentimentalists' were on to something important. Defining man as a brain on legs was severely limiting. A form of beauty that was 'pure spirit' was too ethereal to be of value to most people. A version that provoked strong feelings and emotions, beauty that could be felt as well as observed, was proposed as a new ideal. It would do a better job of engendering our feelings of awe that signal transcendence. This arrangement was, they felt, more 'true' to the complexity of the human individual. Transient or even decaying forms could still provoke glimpses of a reality beyond the quotidian.

Remarkably, this more 'modern' idea flourished, at least among philosophical and artistic types in Western civilizations, throughout the nineteenth century. While the industrial revolution transformed economies and scientific breakthroughs transformed the material world, German thinkers, in particular, spilled a lot of ink articulating how beauty activated non-transactional thinking:

> Beauty is nothing but the beginning of terror, which we are still just able to endure, and we are so awed because it serenely disdains to annihilate us. (Rainer Maria Rilke, *Duino Elegies*)

> [The contemplation of beauty] induces a rapidly alternating repulsion and attraction produced by one and the same object. The point of excess for the imagination... is like an abyss in which it fears to lose itself. (Emanuel Kant, *Critical Philosophy*)

Such provocative and, let's admit it, paradoxical thoughts suggest the idea of 'communion' referenced in discussions of Christianity. The individual, with sufficient concentrated attention on a thing of beauty, may sense a kind of collapse of boundaries. The Germans even invented a word for the experience of such (emotional?) projection: 'empathy' (einfung) which suggests our 'mindmeld' of the self with a loved one.

These Romantics, as they were called, focused on their unique experiences of beauty rather than on universal ideals. They talked of beauty in highly personal, experiential terms. One writer, a French soldier and novelist who was captivated by the art and architecture he discovered in Italy, described his 'mindmeld' encounter with a seventeenth-century work of 'baroque' art[33] in Florence. Lying on his back to contemplate a fresco (of the Sybils by the Italian artist Franceschini, known as Volterrano)

---

[33] The baroque style is characterized by the elaborate use of detail, a kind of 'too much is not enough' elaboration. Think of the Versailles palace or a Bernini fountain.

decorating the ceiling of the Basilica of Santa Croce, he recounts a high level of 'communion' with a spiritual reality:

> Absorbed in contemplating sublime beauty I saw it close up; I touched it so to speak. I had reached that point of emotion where the heavenly sensations of the fine arts meet passionate feeling. As I emerged from Santa Croce, I had palpitations; the life went out of me, and I walked in fear of falling.

The writer, Henri Beyle, known as Stendhal, has lent his name to what is now a syndrome documented in the medical literature. Perhaps he suffered from low blood pressure from lying awkwardly on his back to stare at the ceiling of the church, but similarly powerful experiences have reoccurred in Florence hundreds of times in recent years. A British physician pondered these frequent episodes:

> Art can be so powerful that we forget its unpredictability and faint like Mary at the cross. All those scenes were familiar too to Stendhal whose novels know that in the world of desire a little water is always enough to prime the pump.[34]

So it seems safe to suggest, albeit cautiously, that anyone intent on activating his or her spiritual self could do worse than to invest in seeking beauty. Bringing it into active participation in one's life seems an excellent point of access to the transcendent.

In contemporary terms ideas of beauty have become ever more highly individualistic, not to say idiosyncratic. Thus the seeker of

---

[34] Iain Bamforth, "Stendhal's Syndrome," in the *British Journal of General Practice,* Dec. 2010.

inspiring beauty is obliged to deal with a daunting range of objects and events presented as beautiful. The traditional consensus of what constitutes the 'beautiful' is still on display. Think of all those Renaissance and baroque paintings that look vaguely the same when our untrained eye scans them in room after room in a large state or national museum. As Stendhal testified, these conventional representations of 'beauty' still pack plenty of power to inspire for those willing to get to know them. Anyone lucky enough to see Leonardo's David statue close up will find it hard not to be awestruck. These objects are certainly excellent starting points for an investigation into the transcendent. So too are biographies of exemplary and transformative individuals whose work on behalf of others has the power to inspire imitators— Nelson Mandela, Miep Gies, Martin Luther King, and many others.

But many human creations are no longer 'beautiful' in this conventional sense. Is Duchamp's appropriation of a urinal as an *objet d'art* 'beautiful'? And all those weird Picassos? How does a 'deconstructionist' building by Zaha Hadid stack up against the Pantheon? What about the recently exhibited 'quilts' of Rosie Lee Tomkins compared to traditional American quilts?[35] In light of such a staggering array of productions, from performance art to graffiti, from earth sculpture to concrete poetry, from hip-hop to Erik Satie, how can 'beauty' still be a useful window onto the transcendent? The answer is that it can because, in its diversity, it is able to 'speak' to a larger and more diverse group of seekers. The diversity of makers offers more potential inspirational moments for more people.

---

[35] The uniquely modern quilts of Tomkins were recently exhibited at the UC Berkeley Art Museum. See the review by Roberta Smith in the *New York Times*. https://www.nytimes.com/interactive/2020/06/26/arts/design/rosie-lee-tompkins-quilts.html.

Printed in the United States
by Baker & Taylor Publisher Services